Invisible No More

Ahelia Publishing

Helena, Montana

Invisible No More

Healing Identity: Answering the Call to Arms

Book Two - Personal Identity Restored

Jocelyn Anne Drozda
M.Ed, B.Ed

Invisible—No More
Healing Identity: Answering the Call to Arms
Book Two—Personal Identity Restored

Copyright 2018 Jocelyn Anne Drozda

All rights reserved. No part of this publication may be reproduced, stored in a retrieval system, or transmitted in any form by any process—electronic, mechanical, photocopying, recording, or otherwise—without prior written permission of the copyright owners and Ahelia Publishing, Inc. Any scanning, uploading, and distribution of this book via the Internet or any other means without the permission of the publisher is illegal and punishable by law.

Unless otherwise indicated, all Scriptures are taken from THE HOLY BIBLE, ENGLISH STANDARD VERSION (ESV): Scriptures taken from THE HOLY BIBLE, ENGLISH STANDARD VERSION ® Copyright ©2001 by Crossway, a publishing ministry of Good News Publishers. Used by permission.

Scriptures marked NLT are taken from the HOLY BIBLE, NEW LIVING TRANSLATION (NLT): Scriptures taken from the HOLY BIBLE, NEW LIVING TRANSLATION, Copyright© 1996, 2004, 2007 by Tyndale House Foundation. Used by permission of Tyndale House Publishers, Inc., Carol Stream, Illinois 60188. All rights reserved. Used by permission.

Scriptures marked NKJV are taken from the NEW KING JAMES VERSION (NKJV): Scripture taken from the NEW KING JAMES VERSION®. Copyright© 1982 by Thomas Nelson, Inc. Used by permission. All rights reserved.

ISBN# 978-1-988001-36-4

> Published by Ahelia Publishing, Inc
> Printed in the United States of America
> www.aheliapublishing.com

AHELIA PUBLISHING LLC

Invisible No More
Healing Identity: Answering the Call to Arms

St. Irenaeus[1] is famous for his quote, "The glory of God is man fully alive." I never understood how to become fully alive until I experienced inner healing and deliverance. The tools Jocelyn teaches and guides you with through *Invisible No more* are intentional to minister to your "heart," which is your spirit and soul. To understand how the enemy of our soul, Satan, is out to "steal, kill, and destroy" (John 10:10) every dynamic of our lives is a huge key to understanding how to be fully alive. Jocelyn takes you on a journey to understand how to strengthen your spirit as well as to heal and refresh your soul. Refreshing our soul is an ongoing dynamic of our lives. Just as we must maintain our vehicles by providing tune-ups, oil changes, detailing, checking tire pressure, and washing the exterior of our vehicle, so too, we require maintenance, checking, and cleansing of our "heart."

Our soul is made up of mind, will, and emotions. It is here the enemy launches his attacks upon us through false beliefs, twisted truths, traumas, and brokenness. Jocelyn realized her own need to become "fully alive" and therefore embarked on a journey to discover Truth and to experience the "abundant life" Jesus provides. She realized that maintaining freedom requires applying these tools and techniques on an ongoing basis. This guide will help you to untangle the lies and belief systems the enemy has slyly caused you to believe and will bring healing to your mind through the power of the Holy Spirit and the guidance of Jesus and His Word.

May you be blessed as you begin the greatest adventure of your life—discovering Truth. This book will take you through not only the scriptural truth but also the truth about yourself. This journey will lead you to the freedom and abundant life you have long desired.

Kate Ludwig, Harvest City Church, Canada
Director of Love Lives Here Missions Inc.
Inner Healing and Deliverance Ministry
Cleansing Stream Ministry Leader
Genesis Ministry Leader

▶▶▶This guide can be used individually or with a partner, for small groups or bible studies, and in large group settings. If you are interested in having Jocelyn present a seminar for your retreat or conference, please contact her at:

jdrozda@myaccess.ca

Dedicated to the King of kings that we may be made fit for His service

Sanctified vessels

But in a great house there are not only vessels of gold and silver, but also of wood and clay, some for honor and some for dishonor. Therefore if anyone cleanses himself from the latter, he will be a vessel for honor, sanctified and useful for the Master, prepared for every good work.

2 Timothy 2:20-21 (NKJV)

Table of Contents

My Heart to Yours — Page 8

Book Two—Personal Identity Restored — Page 10

Unit One—Walking Through the Pain (Coping Mechanisms) — Page 11

Unit Two—The Disappearing Act (Self-hatred) — Page 32

Unit Three—The Breach-Wall (Fear) — Page 53

Unit Four—Expectancy (Surrender) — Page 80

Unit Five—Treasure Hunt (Buried Hopes) — Page 98

Unit Six—The Question of Sexuality (Sexuality) — Page 110

Unit Seven—The Enemy's Bitter Fruit (Depression, Anxiety …) — Page 141

Appendix

My Inward Expressions — Page 163

I am Found — Page 165

My Declaration — Page 166

Fully Armed: Worksheet — Page 167

My Healing Testimony — Page 170

Prophetic Voices — Page 171

Recommended Reading — Page 172

Endnotes — Page 173

Endorsements — Page 174

Introducing Book Three—Identity in Christ: Aligned with Destiny — Page 175

My Heart to Yours

We learn best from our mistakes. The Lord knows I have made many. And then I make many more. But through them, I have learned. Oh, how I have learned! And now He has called me to step into the light ... I just didn't realize the complete exposure of me that would happen as I did so. But the Lord has asked me to trust Him, put on a cloak of vulnerability, and become absolutely transparent. In doing so, I have been given the honor of sharing the knowledge with which I have been equipped.

At one time, shame and embarrassment would have stopped me in my tracks from being able to write these words that will put all the messiness of my mind on display. But there is something to be said for opening *all* of our closet doors. The enemy can no longer hold any accusations against you. All his threats are rendered useless as you walk into the light under God's bidding. And there is freedom in that; freedom for both you and me. What once was a weapon of shame in the enemy's hand has become the greatest tool to my freedom ... and hopefully to yours. God loves to turn things on their heads.

When you see yourself healed and changed and you become confident in who you are, in who you are in God, in your relationship with Him, others, and yourself, so many of the things that used to make you feel invisible will no longer matter in the slightest. As the targets come off of your back, the weapons of warfare the enemy had once used against you will be eradicated. The chains set about your wrists and ankles will be cut off, no longer holding you bound.

We are not invisible, unloved, less than, or unworthy. We never have been. It has only been our perception. You are seen by both God and the enemy. God has seen you, known you, and loved you since the beginning of time. Otherwise, He wouldn't have died for you. And He wouldn't be pursuing you. The enemy also sees you and knows you are a danger to him, otherwise he wouldn't have worked so hard all these years to try to make you feel invisible, unloved, and unworthy. And as you learn to walk in the power and authority of your true identity as a child of the Most High God, you become more of a threat. As you expose the darkness—the bad and the ugly in your own life—and bring them before the Father to be forgiven and restored, they get ripped out of the hands of the enemy as weapons. He can no longer accuse you with them, nor hold them over your head as a threat that leads to his control in your life. And eventually, he runs out of weapons and resources to use against you. It is then that he no longer shows up for the fight. It is then that you become unstoppable in the Kingdom of God. It is then that you can walk in the victory of the fight that has already been won by the shed blood of Jesus, the precious Lamb of God.

So take heart; stand strong and courageous. Then take a deep, deep breath. Let's dig in deep and see what the Lord reveals. It will be the journey of your life.

Walk in hope and love, my friend,
Jocelyn Anne Drozda

> And so, from the day we heard, we have not ceased to pray for you, asking that you may be filled with the knowledge of his will in all spiritual wisdom and understanding, so as to walk in a manner worthy of the Lord, fully pleasing to him: bearing fruit in every good work and increasing in the knowledge of God; being strengthened with all power, according to his glorious might, for all endurance and patience with joy; giving thanks to the Father, who has qualified you to share in the inheritance of the saints in light.
> Colossians 1:9-12

Book Two

Personal Identity Restored

… but let your adorning be the hidden person of the heart with the imperishable beauty of a gentle and quiet spirit, which in God's sight is very precious.

1 Peter 3:4

Unit One
Walking Through the Pain

I lift up my eyes to the hills. From where does my help come? My help comes from the LORD, who made heaven and earth. He will not let your foot be moved; he who keeps you will not slumber. Behold, he who keeps Israel will neither slumber nor sleep. The LORD is your keeper; the LORD is your shade on your right hand. The sun shall not strike you by day, nor the moon by night. The LORD will keep you from all evil; he will keep your life. The LORD will keep your going out and your coming in from this time forth and forevermore.

Psalm 121

TIME *DOES NOT* HEAL ALL WOUNDS. IT BURIES THEM; ONLY FOR THEM TO BE EVENTUALLY rediscovered as the pain starts to seep out of our hearts through our thoughts and actions. No, time does not heal pain—we have to jump in and face it head-on. Only through honesty, vulnerability, and exposure of the wounds will come the cleansing and healing from the Lord we so desperately need.

But exposure is hard; too hard we sometimes believe. So instead of walking through the pain head-on, we have created oh so many pathways in attempts to skirt around this confrontation at all costs. And these costs are tremendously high. We sometimes simply numb, consciously or subconsciously shutting down our emotions so we don't feel at all—good or bad. Some seek the aid of drugs, prescription drugs, or alcohol to help them achieve this, and thus get caught in the trap of addictions.

We can make ourselves so busy we do not have time to reflect, think, feel, or deal with anything outside of our own self-prescribed, over-taxed schedules. (This was often my "go-to" method.) This busyness can come in the form of work, projects, hobbies and interests, volunteer commitments, children's activities … Today's society provides endless opportunities for this tactic of avoidance and distraction.

We can create chaos and drama, leaving behind a trail of confusion that keeps us (and everyone around us) so ensnared in the current situation that the underlying source of the problem is overlooked, ignored, or forgotten about.

We can search for the "perfect relationship" that will supposedly heal our hurt, often resulting in a constant succession of unhealthy relationships, only adding more and more turmoil, rejection, and pain to our hearts.

We can choose coping methods of physical gratification to make us temporarily feel better as we attempt to either alleviate the pain or to keep it buried. Unhealthy habits such as overeating, smoking, inappropriate sex, pornography, gambling, and excessive spending can lead to a downward spiral that only results in further negative implications. Our bodies, self-perception, and relationships come to suffer, as these coping methods add another layer of complexity to the underlying issues. (Though they become issues in their own right, they are not the problem, as some are led to believe. If the original pain was healed, the coping mechanisms would no longer be required to disguise the pain.) Shame, condemnation, and self-hatred gang up and complicate the situation even more, and make it extremely difficult to even imagine taking the steps of self-exposure required to bring about healing.

We can also choose one of the various methods of self-harm in misdirected efforts to subdue the pain determined to overwhelm. Though I did not actively pursue this as an adult, I do have an understanding of it, as it had become a battle for me at one point in my life.

When my pain was at its deepest level, I often thought my body would literally explode if it was not alleviated in some way. I desperately wanted to grab a sharp object and slash open my arm … just to let something out, anything out … that would ease the building internal pressure that continually threatened to overtake me, drown me. I fought these thoughts continually for a time. And though I didn't act on them then, I was frustrated and angry with myself that I had even been contemplating it. (But even if I had started cutting, even then, the Lord would have loved me and forgiven me. Any shame and condemnation would be the work of the enemy; that and planting the thoughts of it as a viable method of pain relief in the first place.) I am just thankful the Lord, in preparation for this very battle, had given me what I had needed in advance. It presented itself in almost a warning, happening when I was about 16-years-old.

In the midst of a vulnerable moment during a situation with a friend, I had grabbed a bottle cap and repeatedly scratched the underside of my forearm, breaking through the skin, and creating a six-inch mark. Though it was only a scratch, it scarred, complete with the two visible ridges of the bottle cap. This scar lasted for many, many years, and then slowly faded. Much later, when I was tempted to cut, deeper this time in correlation to such a greater pain, I was reminded of the self-imposed scar I had carried for so many years, and somehow knew I was not to do it again, for this time it would not only scar my body, but my soul.

All of these choices of pain avoidance do not—cannot—lead to health, wholeness, or healing. They are, instead, the pathway to destruction and death. As the internal mind-battle between the pain leaking out and its forced suppression rages on, we can have no peace of mind. Our mental and emotional health are the immediate casualties. And our body can follow suit. The physical strain on it from our own choices and actions, and from stress alone, can lead to disease and terminal illnesses. Our choices of coping methods can also put our bodies in precarious positions that lead to death. And sometimes, we even choose death when we lose all hope that restoration is possible. Whether we act on it or not, even the thoughts of death and destruction can have deadly ramifications as we unconsciously partner with them.

> Pain is good. It is a warning placed in our body or soul to make us take notice something is very wrong.

We, as a society, have learned to avoid pain at any cost—though the cost can be our very lives. **Yet pain is good.** It is a warning placed in our body or soul to make us take notice that something is very wrong—something that we need to take action against before it destroys us. It is *not* a notification for us to take prescription medication, or self-medicate with those deadly coping mechanisms to curb the internal red flags jumping and screaming their SOS. We need to stop masking the symptoms and start healing the internal wounds at their source.

I will not lie to you—the path to healing, walking through your deep, personal pain—is hard. But so is a life filled with dysfunction, addictions, broken relationships, turmoil, and sorrow. Your choice, thus, is not between pain and no pain, hard and easy. The choice is between intense pain for a shorter time as you journey through healing into a life of freedom, and the long-term pain of a life full of avoidance and confusion that leads to death and destruction. You have to ultimately choose your path of pain. I pray the Lord makes your choice clear, my friend.

Pushing Up

A. Exposing Guilt, Shame, and Condemnation

Guilt can be healthy when it urges us to make amends for inappropriate thoughts and actions. After repentance, however, any guilt that still accuses us is not of the Lord. Shame and condemnation creep in by its side and try to silence us, forcing us to keep our heads down and not receive the mercy, grace, and forgiveness of our Heavenly Father, bought by the blood of the Lamb. This guilt, shame, and condemnation also prevent us from receiving the forgiveness of others, which would lead to reconciliation with them. This discord drives a further wedge between us and God, keeping us from feeling like we are the righteous and worthy children of God He says we are, through the death and resurrection of Christ—our true identity.

As a symbolic (prophetic) act, wash your hands and face to remove the veil of guilt, shame, and condemnation. (What you do in obedience in the physical realm will release the healing power in the spiritual realm. This is a method we use in The Cleansing Stream Ministry and I have seen tremendous healing come from this act alone.) You may have to do this step several times through the process until you can lift your eyes to Heaven as you pray to receive forgiveness.

Prayer:

GUILT, SHAME, AND CONDEMNATION I EXPOSE YOU! I CAST YOU OUT AND I REMOVE YOUR VEIL! I will not partner with you any longer. I will not allow you to keep hidden the things which the Lord wants to come to light. My eyes will look to the Lord, where my help comes from. I lift my head and I receive His mercy, His grace, and His forgiveness. I choose to walk in the light of the righteousness that comes from the death and resurrection of Christ Jesus. Father God, I receive Your forgiveness, Your absolution from guilt, shame, and condemnation—all of it. I pray this in Jesus' name. Amen.

B. Pick Your Pain

Indicate which path you choose, by coloring the appropriate box.

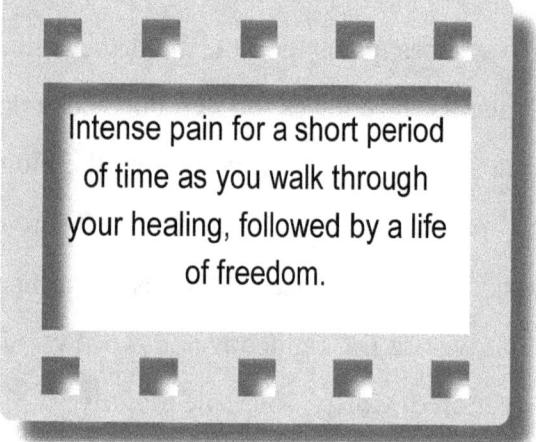

> **Note:** If you struggle in this area, find a trustworthy person to whom you can confess your unhealthy coping mechanisms, and devise a plan for accountability. Having someone stand with you through this process can make a big difference in your success.

C. Examining the Evidence

When pain becomes overwhelming, we often choose various paths of both comfort and avoidance to deal with it or to *not* deal with it.

As you reflect on your life, what destructive patterns do you see emerging as your paths of comforting yourself, and pain avoidance? Record any revelations on the following page.

Remember, healing sometimes needs to come in layers. Return to this section as often as you need.

Prayer:

Holy Spirit, I ask You for the courage and strength I need to prod and stir up this unpleasant area. Please give me revelation and understanding so I can become aware of all the ungodly ways I have chosen to numb my pain, and the negative impact they have had on the different aspects of my life, and the lives of those around me—the ones who have become collateral damage to my poor choices. Help me to be honest and vulnerable, ready and willing to expose all that You wish to be exposed at this time. I surrender them all to You, Lord! I choose to stop running. I choose to turn around and face it head-on, like the mighty, brave warrior I am!

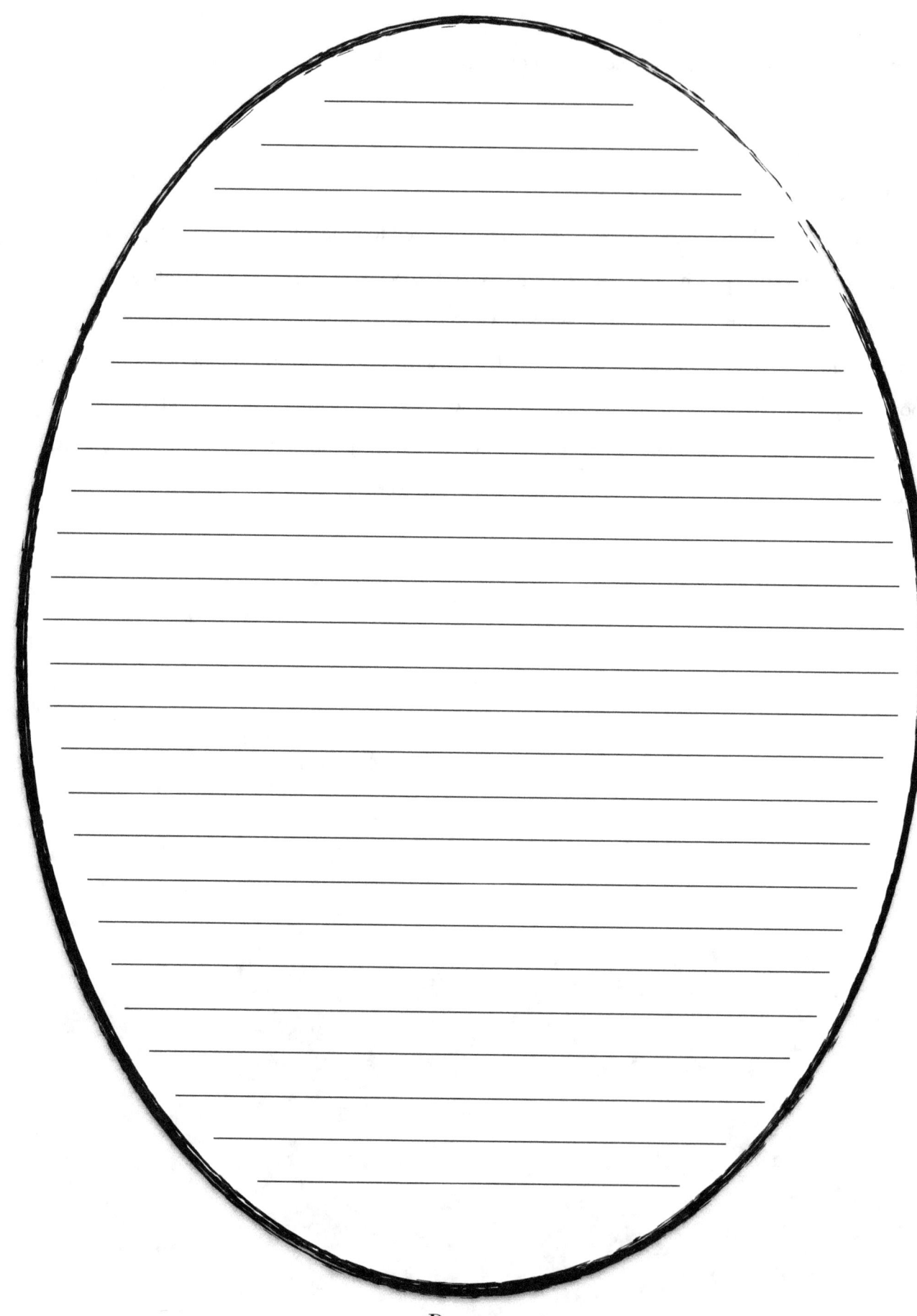

D. Assessing Collateral Damage

The choices we make when we bury our issues rather than confronting them always have a negative impact on our lives and the lives of those around us.

What has been the impact of the coping methods you have chosen on you and on all those with whom you are in relationship?

_____
_____
_____
_____
_____
_____
_____

E. Gaining Freedom Through Repentance

The Lord would have us go to Him for all of our needs, especially those of our suffering. Repentance opens the door to His mercy and healing grace.

Write a prayer of repentance for all of the ways in which you have chosen to handle or avoid handling the pain you have suffered, instead of opening up in vulnerability and taking it to the Father. Bring before Him all those you have hurt through your negative choices and decisions. Pray a blessing over them.

Forgive yourself. Remember, you did the best you could with what you had at the time.
Receive His forgiveness. (Use the information from Part D to guide your prayer of repentance.)
Is there anyone from whom you need to ask for personal forgiveness or need to make restitution?

F. Walking in Alignment

It is time to come out of alignment with any of the lies or inner vows under which you have been operating. These lies and vows could include areas such areas as *justifying the pain avoidance, denying its devastating implications on you and on those with whom you are in relationship*, and those of shame that may *continue to threaten you not to expose*, or even *withdraw that which you have already exposed.* The lies may sound like: "I have to ... It is not hurting anyone... No one has to know ... There is no other way I can survive ... It is not really that bad ... I can't handle things without it ... Just one more time ... I can handle it ... I will *always* ... I will *never* ..."

Pray to break off the lies and inner vows and come out of alignment with them. Realign yourself with God's truth. Take time to listen to the voice of Holy Spirit for revelation of both the lies and God's truth.

Prayer:

Dear Lord, I ask that You take Your dagger—Your sword of the Spirit—and dig out all the lies and inner vows I have made that are keeping me from walking in the light, in my true identity. Reveal to me Your truth in which I need to walk. I ask for the unwavering steadfastness and resolve that it will take for me to stand strong through this painful process as it unfolds over this next part of my journey. Holy Spirit, please reveal to me the lies of the enemy and the truth of who You originally created me to be, as I lay my heart exceedingly bare before You.

I come out of alignment with the lie that says _____.

This is not the truth. Your truth says _____.

I come out of alignment with the lie that says _____.

This is not the truth. Your truth says _____.

I come out of alignment with the lie that says _____.

This is not the truth. Your truth says _____.

G. Grieving Things Lost

We suffer great losses during the times we have been embroiled in this battle for our souls. Some things we lose can never be replaced: family, friends, careers, time, opportunity, health, Kingdom purpose … We have much to grieve. What have you lost?

Prayer:

Dear Lord,

My heart grieves for all I have lost because of the situations I have been in, the choices I have made, and the negative choices those around me have made. Though some things cannot be replaced, Lord, You can restore them. You can restore my future. You can give me a hope. You can restore me and those around me. Carry my heart, Lord, as I walk through the sadness of grief.

I have lost:

I give all of this to You, Lord. Bind up the wounds and holes these losses have caused in my heart. Fill the spaces with Your healing balm, Your love, Your mercies and grace. I can't do this without You. Please stay by my side that I may rest in You. I ask You, Lord, to show me what is in Your heart for me at this very moment in the depth of my sadness. **Record His revelations in words and pictures.**

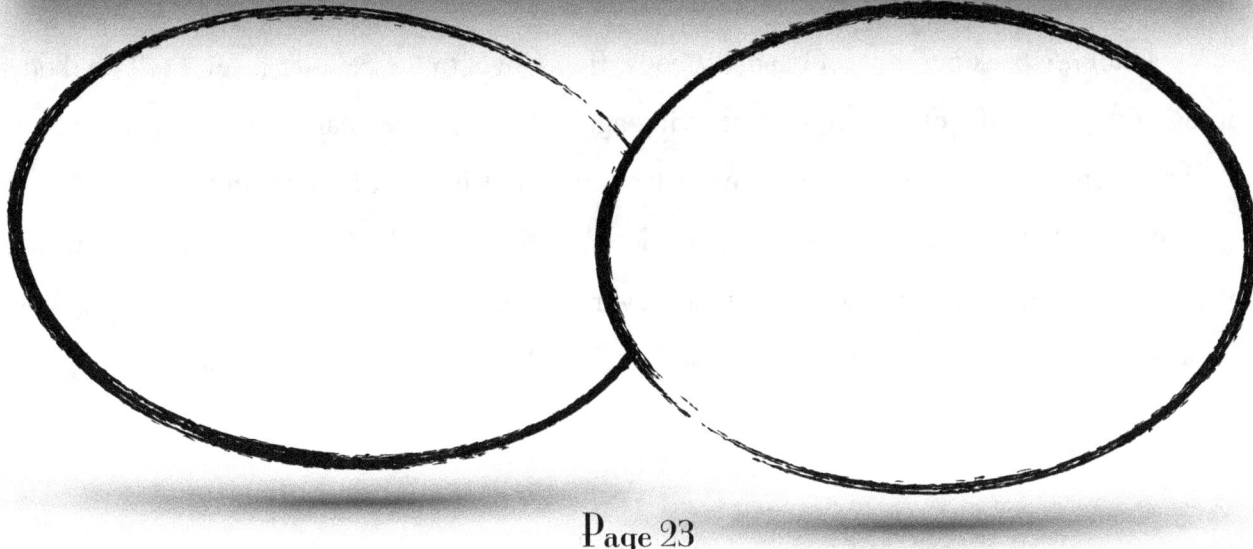

H. Breaking the Power of Chaos, Death, and Destruction

As we engage in behaviors that reflect despair and hopelessness and that are detrimental to our being or that of those around us, we are, in essence, choosing to partner with the spirit of death and destruction. As things fall into turmoil and disorder all around us, it is the spirit of chaos at work.

Pray to come out of alignment with the power of chaos, death, and destruction in your life. Then pray to bring healing and to restore order, life, hope, and blessing.

Prayer:
SPIRIT OF CHAOS, I CAST YOU OUT, IN THE NAME OF JESUS! I will not partner with you any longer. I cancel every assignment to bring disorder into my life in my spirit, mind, body, household, and every aspect of my life, and that of those around me. I come out of agreement with all thoughts, actions, and patterns in my life that do not reflect the peace and order of God. I ask You, Lord, to bring godly order to all areas of my life that are in disarray.

SPIRIT OF DEATH AND DESTRUCTION, IN JESUS' NAME I TAKE AUTHORITY OVER YOU AND I CAST YOU OUT! I do not permit you to kill, steal, and destroy my life, or any of the lives of those around me. I remove from you all power over my life. I cancel your reign, and I take down all strongholds you have built. I come out of agreement with all thoughts, actions, and behaviors that lead to death.

I call *life* back into my soul and my body, right down to the cellular level. I tell my body, through the power of Holy Spirit, to start living again. Lord, please heal every place in my body that has been damaged due to the trauma I have incurred in my life, and any damage I have willfully inflicted on myself through my choices. In the name of Jesus, I reverse all muscle memory that entered during times of trauma. Rewire my brain, Lord, to operate as You originally intended it—with order, from a place of rest. Lord, fill me with life, hope, and peace. I step into joy. I ask for Your blessings and strength as I continue down this path toward complete spiritual, mental, emotional, and physical health. I pray this in the holy name of Jesus. Amen.

I. Releasing Protective Personalities

We often develop *protective personalities** to help us accomplish our pain avoidance strategies. As long as they are prevalent in our thought patterns, they will continue to control our reactions and behaviors and keep us enmeshed in pain avoidance. These false personalities are not in line with who God says we are and therefore are not a part of our personal identity. It is time to release them and to ask Jesus to help us not only cope, but to walk surrounded by true peace and joy.

Read through the list of common protective personalities. Highlight the ones with which you identify. Add to the list if necessary. Release them, following the sample prayer. You may have to return to this section periodically throughout your healing journey as further protective personalities are revealed.

(*From The Genesis Process[2]. Used with permission.)

			Other:
✦ Doormat	✦ Blank	✦ The Phony	
✦ Nice	✦ Numb	✦ The Perfectionist	✦ _____
✦ The Pleaser	✦ The Martyr	✦ The Victim	✦ _____
✦ Anger	✦ The Protector	✦ Control	✦ _____
✦ The Bully	✦ The Intimidator	✦ Needy	✦ _____
✦ I'm ok	✦ The Rescuer	✦ Don't mess with me	✦ _____
✦ Over Achiever	✦ Invisible	✦ The Wall	✦ _____
✦ Confusion	✦ The Critic	✦ Independence	

Prayer:

Holy Spirit, please show me the traps of the enemy that I have fallen into, believing that they were a part of my personality; believing they have kept me safe. Lord God, I repent of operating in these behaviors. I do not want them to be a part of my life. I will no longer identify with them. I release _____ (name of protective personality) from my life. I will not partner with it any longer. I don't want it. I don't need it. It is not a part of my God-given identity. I ask You, Lord Jesus, instead, to guard me against any wounding in this area I have been guarding against. I repent of any wounding I have caused others as I operated under this false identity. Thank You, Jesus, for protecting me and keeping me safe. (Continue to release all of the highlighted protective personalities.)

J. Releasing Judgments

The judgments we make on others will become the judgments made against us. Matthew 7:1-2 says, "Judge not, that you be not judged. For with the judgment you pronounce you will be judged, and with the measure you use it will be measured to you." Often, we have chosen coping methods to hide or soothe the deep pain others have inflicted upon us through their individual behavior and how they have treated us. We then hold a judgment against them. This puts a target on our back, as it opens a spiritual door that allows the enemy to tempt us to do to others the very things we held against the one who did them to us. (We do the very things that were done to us.)

The time has come to release these ones on whom you have passed judgment and come to a place of forgiveness. Be assured, you do not have to put them in a position of trust, nor do you have to condone what they have done. You are just removing them from your judgment, and leaving it in the hands of the One who is more than able to complete this task. This not only releases them from your hooks in the spiritual realm but also releases you from captivity. You cannot heal as you hold the blackness of unforgiveness in your heart.

Prayer:

Dear Holy Spirit, Giver of truth and revelation, I ask You to please reveal to me any people I am holding in judgment—the ones known to me, and the deep ones, that perhaps I have not even admitted to myself. (Give time for Holy Spirit revelation.)

I bring before you _____.
I repent for holding them under my judgment. It is not my place to judge them; it is Yours and Yours alone. I remove all spiritual hooks I have placed in them and release them from all of my judgments, also releasing myself as I do so. I forgive them for all of the wrongs I feel they have done to me. I break off all soul ties I have with them, and I give them completely over to You. I also ask for Your forgiveness for any negative part I have played in every encounter I have had with them. I receive Your forgiveness and proclaim my freedom. I pray this in Jesus' name.

K. Unheard Apology for Those Abused

Often, our hearts cry out to be heard. When we feel heard, the pain can be released a little easier. We want those who hurt us to know they have hurt us, abused us, betrayed us. But those hurt ones who hurt us do not always hear the cries of our hearts. But know, dear friend, the deep cries of your heart are heard. And on behalf of those who hurt you, I offer my heart in regret, and I pray the words of Calli Linwood[3], who knows what you know, and has felt what you have felt, will comfort you.

Abuse... nasty stuff. It is one of those things that you truly don't understand the depths of its destruction until you have walked in it. Don't say, "It wasn't that bad." You only feel this way if you know no other way anymore. Like a frog in boiling water, you get used to the turmoil; forgetting it will eventually take its deathly toll. Don't say, "It was really my fault, I pushed him (her)." No matter what you did, no matter what you said, it did not warrant the exaggerated violent response nor the awful words that forced their way into your soul, coloring it black.

It is not right what happened to you. It is not just. It is not fair. You bore the brunt of another's shame, of another's pain, of another's anger as he (she) lashed back at the world. You were caught in the crossfire of a fight that was not your own. You were bruised, either on the surface or deep in your heart; it makes no difference which. Both inflict the same kind of wound. You ache for some acknowledgment that what happened to you was not right, not just, not fair. But you never hear the words. Or, you have learned not to trust them, for they are just another sandcastle on the beach, anyway.

But I know what happened to you is not right, not just, not fair. **It is not right. It is not just. It is not fair.** And so on behalf of this person who did this to you, I am truly and deeply sorry. I am sorry for your hurt. I am sorry for your pain. I am sorry for everything that your poor heart had to carry for all this time. I am sorry for each day you had to struggle through, feeling like you were going to break. I am truly sorry that in all the places and circumstances where you should have received love, joy, affection and honor, you instead were stripped bare; robbed of all that should have been given to you. I am sorry I did not stop what was being done to you. I am sorry that I did not listen; that I left you as one of the voiceless ones. I am sorry I did not help you. I am truly, deeply sorry.

Now I ask for your forgiveness, so your heart can be set free. You deserve that. You deserve to move forward in life with pure joy that comes from a heart that has been fully healed. And your heart can be healed; if only you open it enough to let the pain out and let God's grace come in. Be brave. You can do this.

(From the book *Break Forth: Becoming victorious over a past of abuse, trauma and domestic violence*, by Calli Linwood. Used with permission.)

His Truth

Speak the truth of the Holy Scriptures out loud. Let each promise of God soak into every place in your heart to bring you comfort.

"You are my servant, I have chosen you and not cast you off"; fear not, for I am with you; be not dismayed, for I am your God; I will strengthen you, I will help you, I will uphold you with my righteous right hand.

Isaiah 41:9b-10

For God alone, O my soul, wait in silence, for my hope is from him. He only is my rock and my salvation, my fortress; I shall not be shaken.

Psalm 62:5-6

For sin will have no dominion over you, since you are not under law but under grace.

Romans 6:14

He sent out his word and healed them, and delivered them from their destruction.

Psalm 107:20

He himself bore our sins in his body on the tree, that we might die to sin and live to righteousness. By his wounds you have been healed.

1 Peter 2:24

And because you belong to him, the power of the life-giving Spirit has freed you from the power of sin that leads to death.

Romans 8:2 (NLT)

The LORD is my shepherd; I shall not want.

Psalm 23:1

The thief comes only to steal and kill and destroy. I came that they may have life and have it abundantly. I am the good shepherd. The good shepherd lays down his life for the sheep.

John 10:10-11

Submit yourselves therefore to God. Resist the devil, and he will flee from you. Draw near to God, and he will draw near to you.

James 4:7-8a

Therefore, confess your sins to one another and pray for one another, that you may be healed. The prayer of a righteous person has great power as it is working.

James 5:16

As it is, I rejoice, not because you were grieved, but because you were grieved into repenting. For you felt a godly grief, so that you suffered no loss through us. For godly grief produces a repentance that leads to salvation without regret, whereas worldly grief produces death.

2 Corinthians 7:9-10

Praying His Truth

Call on the Lord for His help in fighting this battle by praying His Word.

Thank You, Lord, for being my Good Shepherd, who has laid down His life for me, that I may have abundant life. Thank You, that because I belong to You, the power of the life-giving Spirit has freed me from the power of sin that leads to death. In You, I am free from the bondage of sin. I speak that now over my life. Lead me into a godly grief that I may be led into repentance in all areas of my life that are still being held hostage. Expose the truth, in Jesus' name. Thank You for the salvation that comes with repentance. Help me die to sin in all areas of my life, that I may live to righteousness; You give power to the prayer of the righteous. I desire the power of the righteous, that I may partner with You, Lord, to bring reconciliation of Your people, to You.

I pray that by the power of Your grace, sin no longer has dominion over me; I submit myself to you. Help me to resist the devil, especially in those areas of my weaknesses. Make him flee from me, O Lord! I choose to draw near to You, as You have chosen me, and do not cast me off. Strengthen me! Help me! Uphold me with Your righteous right hand! Deliver me from destruction! I do not fear, as You are with me, my God. By Your Word, by Your wounds, You heal me. Bring this healing to me, please, in every area of my life—body, soul, and spirit. I wait for You, Lord, and You alone. My hope is in You. You are my rock and my salvation.

You are my fortress.

In You, I shall not be shaken.

The Lord is my shepherd. I shall not want.

Unit Two
The Disappearing Act

IMAGINE YOU ARE WEARING THOSE CLOTHES—YOU KNOW, THE ONES YOU PERHAPS HAD TO wear for your Christmas photos as a kid or as a requirement at work—the ones that are extremely uncomfortable, scratchy, rubbing you raw, screaming for you to take them off so you can stop feeling the constant irritation, even pain. Now imagine that you can't—can't take them off—ever —because it is not the clothes—it is you—your body. Welcome to the last forty-some years of my life. It has not been fun to never be at peace in my own body.

The neurologist calls it Tourettes. I didn't because I never wanted to take that on as my identity, to claim it, to make it more a part of me than it already had been. I just called it hateful.

The almost never-ending buildup of tension in my body could only be relieved by a rolling of the shoulder or the belly, a sniff, blink, squint, or some other odd facial grimace or body contortion. But the relief would only last mere seconds and force me to do it again and again, even past the point when my joints, swollen and inflamed, made it sheer agony to do so.

And then suddenly, the need to perform that particular movement would disappear, with or without a time of reprieve, and I'd move on to the next awkward "habit," only for the former one to resurface again at a later time. Only they weren't habits, and if I could "just stop" or substitute a more socially acceptable, less obvious movement … I probably would have eventually figured that out! I did not dictate the tics and twitches—they dictated me.

Growing up, and even as an adult, this condition caused more damage to my identity than anything else in my life, and I admit, I have not handled it at all gracefully nor godly. The fact that I could not control it was an intense source of shame. I felt like a failure, as I could not even control my own body. As smart, capable, and accomplished as I came to be, I still could not control the most basic of things … something even most children can do. This proved to be more than humiliating on many occasions. I also always felt this affliction was just so unfair in that it was just so pointless. The whole condition just didn't make sense to me or to others. If I was in a wheelchair, people would understand that I couldn't "just get up." This, they don't understand. *I didn't understand.*

Up until the past few years, I would almost never talk about this affliction, even with my best friends or family, and I would hate, with an intense passion, anyone who mocked me, teased me, or even mentioned it. I would avoid that person, lie about it, and if at all possible, shut down the relationship. It had been a huge source of frustration and embarrassment over my lifetime, overshadowing most of my positive accomplishments and attributes. My sister always whined that I was the pretty one. Yet when people stared at me, and they did, sometimes many at once while pointing it out to others, they were not noticing what I looked like but were only waiting to see if I *did it again*. And I never disappointed them, try as I could to suppress the tics. It had led me to believe, *What good was it to be pretty when you always did such weird things?*

I grew extremely self-conscious about how I appeared to others, and this was only magnified as photos and videos would catch me in a horrid grimace. I eventually avoided video cameras when at all possible, and even opted not to have my wedding recorded.

This negative view of myself, both in how I felt and how I saw myself, was a pervasive force that formed much of my false identity. In fact, it made me want to disappear. And in doing so, I placed my own cloak of invisibility over my head and did just that. I chose to be unseen. And though I didn't really understand this at the time, I put a huge enemy target on my back that rendered the door wide open to his ruthless attacks, and gave him the power to do it.

I saw myself as a freak. I hated it. I hated myself. And I hated God for making me like that. It was my one *untouchable* area. I *could* not, *would* not talk about it. Even as I dug deeper into the emotional healing I needed to deal with the other traumas I had incurred over my lifetime, I avoided talking about this area as much as possible, only briefly acknowledging it, effectively skimming over it when it reared its ugly head and refused to be ignored. The longer I could keep it at bay, pretend it didn't exist, pretend I wasn't *that* person, the longer I could keep the *"freak identity"* from surfacing. In daily life I could ignore it at times, refusing to think about how I must look to others, even though the way I felt was a constant reminder. But generally, it was always there, infiltrating my mind and heart, lying to me that I would always be on the outside of life. I do know, in the midst of it all, there was a great measure of God's grace, or I would not have been able to do all that I have done in my life, or put myself in the positions I have over the years. And for this I am thankful.

But, as much as I avoided facing this part of myself, it had to surface, really surface, if this part of my false identity was to be healed. Healing is funny that way. Things have to be fully exposed before they can be healed. As hard as it is to confront and deal with some things, our "untouchable" things, it always works this way. Once things are exposed, they lose their power to control us. We need to consciously put them on the altar, no matter how hateful or shameful we find them, no matter how deeply we've buried them, no matter how much we hate them, hate ourselves, or hate

> Once something is exposed, it loses its power to control us. We need to put everything on the altar.

God because of them. It is only then the healing can begin.

So God, in His mercy and grace, (only it definitely did not feel like mercy and grace at the time), would begin to bring up my *untouchable* area of self-hatred again and again, in front of an ever-widening audience. And I was so angry with Him for doing it. And I so love Him for doing it. The fact that I can now fully expose this torment of my mind and body in black and white for the whole world to see, with only slightly more than a minimal twist of my gut, is a testament to how much healing I have received in this area.

It was through this process that I finally became strong and brave enough to confront the Lord about it, confessing to Him my hatred for myself, and my hatred for how He had made me. His response, however, was completely unexpected and left me dumbfounded.

"I didn't make you like that. It is an imperfection caused by the infiltration of the enemy in the fallen world."

This meant He did not create me with this affliction; it was not a part of my original design … yet for all these years I had been blaming Him. In shock, I immediately repented for my accusations against Him, and for speaking, thinking, and partnering with the lie, "I am a freak." And then, I was able to redirect my thinking and begin to seek the Lord for my complete healing and restoration.

There are some things, however, that we may hate about ourselves that *were* a part of our original creation. This too, can be healed as He shifts our perspective and helps us to accept that part of ourselves, simply because He intentionally chose to create us in that manner, for His unique purposes. And He, Himself, loves that very thing about us.

For me, this thing I hated about myself was my voice, both talking and singing. I literally cringed when I heard myself on a recording, and I became extremely embarrassed when I had to listen to myself in the presence of others. I tried to avoid being in that circumstance at all costs!

Driving in my vehicle one day, loudly singing to the Lord in worship, I actually apologized to Him for the fact that He was forced to listen to my horrible voice. He softly whispered to my soul, "I love hearing you sing to Me." His words immediately shifted my perspective. I wept and was healed from this self-hatred. He reaffirmed this in me with a Scripture and supportive words from two friends a short time later. This solidified my healing, and it has never bothered me since. (O my darling, lingering in the gardens, your companions are fortunate to hear your voice. Let me hear it too! Song of Songs 8:13 NLT.)

Pushing Up

A. Ripping off the Bandaid

Self-hatred can originate from both internal and external sources. It can stem from physical aspects such as your facial features, body, voice, race, family, gender, and sexuality, or aspects about yourself, such as your personality, characteristics, skills, and abilities. It can be birthed from things that have happened to you, have been said to you, things you've done or said, or even things you have failed to do or say.

Self-hatred may be so obvious it mockingly shrieks at you from the mirror every day, or so heavily shrouded, so deeply guarded—*untouchable*—that you barely acknowledge it. Yet its impact, known or unknown, is like a tidal wave. **Present this issue to the Lord in prayer to begin the process of exploration.**

Prayer:

Dear God, You know me better than I know myself. I cannot hide anything from You; You know it all, anyway. Please unveil the layers that keep those areas about myself under wraps, hidden from others; even perhaps, hidden from me. I need to confront and get to the heart of this issue, for in doing so, it will release me to get to my own heart—all of it, so it can be healed, restored, and then filled and overflowing with love for You, for others, and for myself.

I ask You to reveal the root of this issue—when, where, and how it came in, and what experiences have continued to reinforce any lies to which I have attached myself. I shut the mouth of the enemy, and take his hands off of my ears. I ask for complete revelation and clarity to hear Your voice. And I ask for courage, so I can boldly and unashamedly walk full force into this healing arena and come out victorious, with You by my side. I pray this in Jesus' name.

✦ **What is your self-hatred?**

_____
_____
_____
_____
_____
_____
_____
_____
_____

This is God's truth of how he made you and how He sees you.

> So God created man in his own image, in the image of God he created him; male and female he created them. And God saw everything that he had made, and behold, it was very good.
>
> **Genesis 1:27, 31a**
>
> For we are God's masterpiece. He has created us anew in Christ Jesus, so we can do the good things he planned for us long ago.
>
> **Ephesians 2:10 (NLT)**

B. Digging Out the Dirt

Answer each question that is relevant to your situation and any Holy Spirit asks of you. This section takes the courage for which you have asked, as it will hurt. But the pain must come out so infection and all its poison does not set in, and that which is already there can be cleansed. Be sure to take time in between the questions to listen to Holy Spirit. Work in conjunction with Him, and He will reveal the areas that need to be explored. Do not ignore the things that are at the back of your mind, but ask Holy Spirit to bring them into the light.

✦ **What damage has this issue of self-hatred brought to your identity?**

_____
_____
_____
_____
_____
_____

✦ **What names did you call yourself? What words did you speak over yourself?**

_____
_____
_____
_____
_____
_____

◆ **What did other people say about you? What words were spoken over you by others?**

_____
_____
_____
_____
_____

◆ **What actions were taken against you by yourself or others?**

_____
_____
_____
_____
_____

◆ **What other experiences have occurred to reinforce your self-hatred?**

_____
_____
_____
_____
_____
_____

✦ **How have you conducted yourself as a response to self-hatred?** Did you ignore or pretend, put on a mask, play a charade, lash out in anger, isolate, act out behaviors rejecting self, others or God …

_____
_____
_____
_____
_____
_____
_____
_____

✦ **What have been the results of this behavior? What have you lost because of it? How has your life and the lives of those around you been impacted because of it?**

_____
_____
_____
_____
_____
_____
_____
_____

✦ **What lies have you been believing about yourself?**

_____
_____
_____
_____
_____
_____
_____
_____
_____

✦ **What vows did you make to yourself, thinking they would keep you safe?** (*I will never/always…*) Remember to continually work with Holy Spirit during this process.

_____
_____
_____
_____
_____
_____
_____
_____

In response to self-hatred, we consciously or subconsciously cover ourselves in the natural and the emotional, but also in the spiritual. This can result in a spiritual cloak that not only disguises our true God-given identity but attempts to destroy it and sabotage our full destiny in Christ.

Did you put on a cloak to cover up your self-hatred? Was it a cloak of Invisibility? Unworthiness? Unlovability? Silence? Arrogance? Pride? Anger? Envy? False humility? Inferiority? Suppression? ...

Prayer:

Dear Lord, in my shame of self-hatred I may have masked my true, God-given identity, covering it up with a self-imposed cloak. Holy Spirit, please reveal any cloaks with which I have covered myself: _____

C. Cleansing the Wound

What is the root of the self-hatred? When, where, and how did self-hatred come into your life? Pray for Holy Spirit to specifically show you this. Be still before Him, listening to His voice. **Record His revelations to you.**

_____
_____
_____
_____
_____
_____
_____
_____

Prayer:

Lord Jesus, please show me where You were when this event happened that opened the door to self-hatred, causing such woundedness. Show me how You were with me and how You helped me. (Give time for this revelation, then record it.)

_____
_____
_____
_____
_____
_____
_____
_____
_____
_____
_____

Lord, I close and seal this door in the name of Jesus! I ask You to heal my wound and soothe my heart. Remove any trauma stored in my body that was deposited during this event.

On a separate piece of paper, write all the false-identity names you have called yourself and others have called you. Add any word curses or lies you have spoken over yourself and that were spoken over you, and any inner vows you have made. Use the previous pages for reference. Write the *opposite* of everything you write in the space below.

Now burn, rip, shred, crumple, or otherwise destroy the paper and forcibly declare:

I AM COMING OUT OF ALIGNMENT WITH THESE WORDS—ALL VOWS AND LIES—AND THEY WILL NO LONGER CONTROL ANY ASPECT OF MY LIFE! I TAKE BACK MY LIFE! I BREAK ALL COVENANTS, VOWS, AND AGREEMENTS I HAVE MADE THAT DO NOT LINE UP WITH THE WORD OF THE LORD AND WHO HE SAYS I AM—WHO HE CREATED ME TO BE! I TAKE OFF THE CLOAK OF _____. (Take off the cloak in the physical as a prophetic act.) I RIP ALL ENEMY TARGETS OF SELF-HATRED OFF OF MY BACK. (Do it!) I BREAK THEIR POWER OVER ME. FROM THIS MOMENT FORWARD, I FORBID ACCESS TO MY HEART THROUGH THE PATH OF SELF-HATRED! I REVERSE ALL MUSCLE MEMORY AND BRAIN PATHWAYS THAT KEEP ME BOUND. I WILL BOLDLY AND UNAPOLOGETICALLY WALK IN EXACTLY WHO THE LORD CREATED ME TO BE! MY HEART BELONGS TO THE LORD! I SPEAK LIFE INTO MY SOUL! I WILL INSTEAD BELIEVE … (Read the words written in the box on the previous page, firmly and resolutely. Perform any prophetic acts which the Holy Spirit requests of you.)

D. Dressing the Wound

God created you and He loves His creation. He loves you. Should we not love *all* he has created as well, including ourselves? Repentance brings resolution and freedom.

Ask the Lord to bring your heart to a place of repentance for not loving yourself, and for not taking care of yourself—for not honoring His creation (in the exact form it is in right now, whether it is in its original design or not). He loves you so dearly, *right now!*

Pour your heart out as you write a prayer asking God for forgiveness. Your prayer may address such areas as rebellion, hating God's creation, hating, judging, or blaming God, believing He is not good, partnering with the lies of self-hatred, not believing He loves you, negative thoughts, actions, and behaviors that were in response to self-hatred, and burying or masking the issues instead of bringing them to the Lord in trust of His faithfulness. **Take some time at the end to give thanks. A grateful heart brings healing.**

What Scripture resonates in your heart that indicates the love Father God has for you?

E. Healing the Scar

What have you lost by being bound in self-hatred all these years?

_____

Take some time to grieve these things and ask the Lord to heal and seal Your heart. Ask Him to restore to you in double portion all you have lost by this deception of the enemy.

Ask the Lord if He indeed created you this way, or if it was created by the fallen world, or even by your own beliefs, actions, behaviors, and choices.

_____

What do you need to do in response to His revelation? Is there something you can do to change the actual circumstances of your self-hatred? What is your part in your restoration? *Ask Him for further revelation and direction for healing and restoration.* Do you need Him to shift your perspective and help you to accept and embrace that part of yourself? *Ask Him to show you how He loves that very thing about you, His purposes in it, and how you can walk in it in a way that is pleasing to Him—in a manner that will advance His Kingdom.*

Ask the Lord to reveal His perspective on the things you have hated about yourself. Record the revelations of His perspective of you—how He sees you—on the next page.

I am God's Masterpiece

Both exactly as I am right here, right now …
and how He is making me to be. Thank You for both versions of me,
And everything in between.
This is how the Lord God, Creator of the heavens,
Creator of ME, sees me …

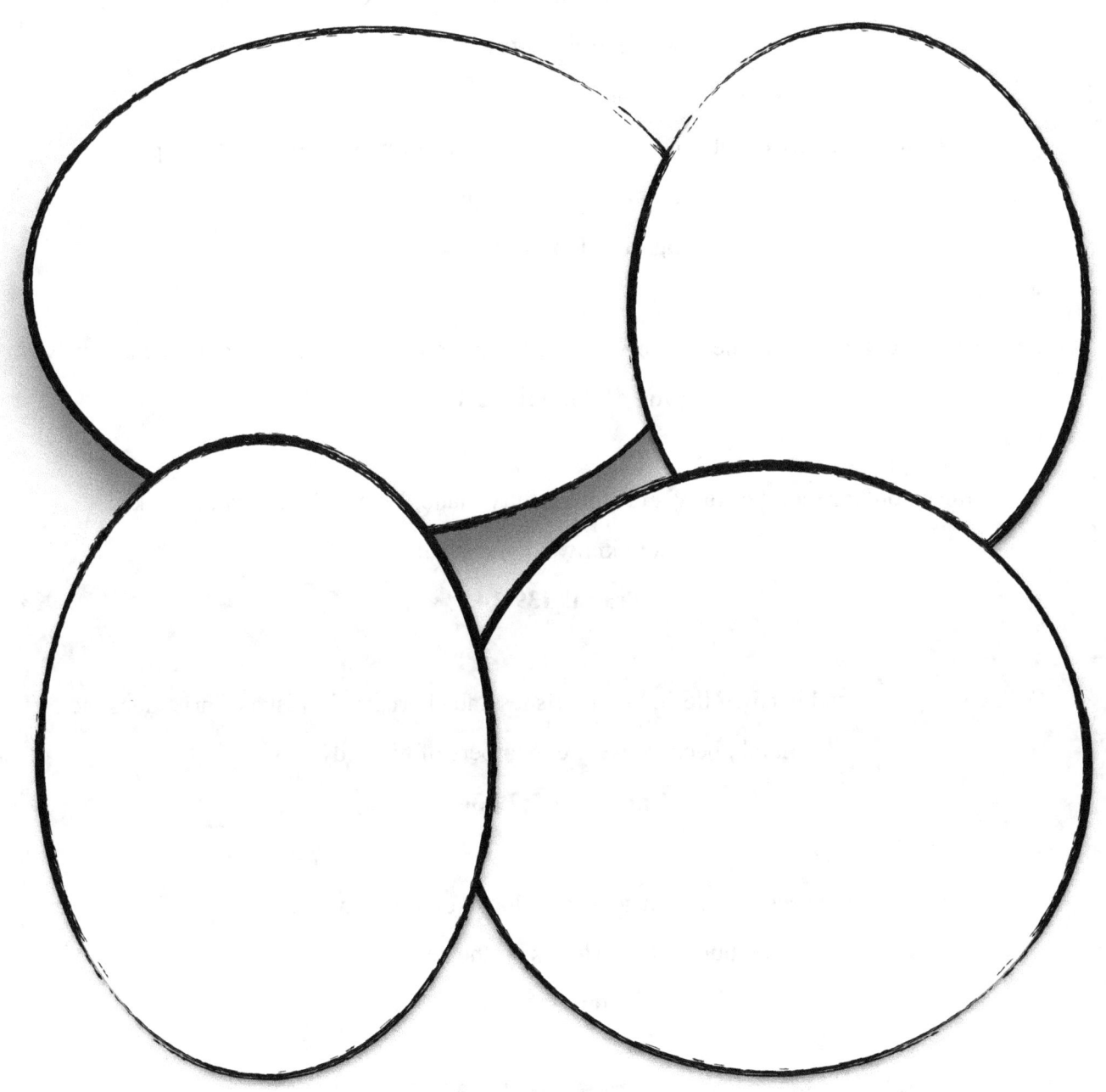

His Truth

Speak the truth of God's Word to see how He sees you and to shift your perspective.

He has made everything beautiful in its time.

Ecclesiastes 3:11a

You are altogether beautiful, my love; there is no flaw in you.

Song of Solomon 4:7

"Arise, my love, my beautiful one, and come away, for behold, the winter is past;

the rain is over and gone.

Song of Solomon 2:10b-11

… let me see your face, let me hear your voice, for your voice is sweet, and your face is lovely.

Song of Solomon 2:14b

I praise you, for I am fearfully and wonderfully made. Wonderful are your works;

my soul knows it very well.

Psalms 139:14

For no one ever hated his own flesh, but nourishes and cherishes it, just as Christ does the

church, because we are members of his body.

Ephesians 5:29-30

For the LORD sees not as man sees: man looks on the outward appearance,

but the LORD looks on the heart.

1 Samuel 16:7b

"They shall be Mine," says the LORD of hosts,

"On the day that I make them My jewels.

Malachi 3:17a (NKJV)

The second is this: 'You shall love your neighbor <u>as yourself</u>.'

There is no other commandment greater than these."

Mark 12:31

Whoever gets sense loves his own soul; he who keeps understanding will discover good.

Proverbs 19:8

… but let your adorning be the hidden person of the heart with the imperishable beauty of a gentle and quiet spirit, which in God's sight is very precious.

1 Peter 3:4

So to keep me from becoming conceited because of the surpassing greatness of the revelations, a thorn was given me in the flesh, a messenger of Satan to harass me, to keep me from becoming conceited. Three times I pleaded with the Lord about this, that it should leave me. But he said to me, "My grace is sufficient for you, for my power is made perfect in weakness." Therefore I will boast all the more gladly of my weaknesses, so that the power of Christ may rest upon me. For the sake of Christ, then, I am content with weaknesses, insults, hardships, persecutions, and calamities. For when I am weak, then I am strong.

2 Corinthians 12:7-10

Declaring His Truth

Make these scriptural declarations out loud. Know that this is how the Lord sees you. Let this truth settle deep into your heart. Add your own declarations. Repeat this often.

> The Lord has made everything beautiful—I am beautiful!
>
> He sees no flaw in me; to Him, I am perfect in Jesus.
>
> My spring has come; I will arise and come away with the Lord,
>
> as He loves me and wants to spend time with me.
>
> My voice is sweet, my face is lovely. This is how the Lord sees me.
>
> I am fearfully and wonderfully made—in every detail,
>
> for the work of the Lord is wonderful.
>
> I cherish and nourish my flesh, just as Christ does, because I am a member of His body.
>
> The Lord sees my heart and loves my heart. It is the heart of man that matters.
>
> I will no longer look on outward appearances; I too, will see and understand man—and myself—as the Lord intended us to see—looking upon the heart. It is my heart that matters. It is the hearts of those around me that matter. I belong to the Lord; I am His. He has made me His jewel, His treasured possession, His special treasure.
>
> I shall love my neighbor as I love myself—I will love myself so I can be faithful to love my neighbor as the Lord asks of me. I will discover good as I learn to love my own soul more and more. As I bring my soul in quiet reverence to the Lord, the Lord will grant me His imperishable beauty, which is precious in His sight.
>
> The Lord's grace is sufficient for me. His power is made perfect in weakness.
>
> When I am weak, then I am strong, as the power of Christ rests upon me.
>
> This is how the Lord sees me. I rest in His grace.

Unit Three
The Breach-Wall

Prophetic word - May 2017

The first thing I saw was a very dark wave ... just boiling, churning—dark and tumultuous ... like a huge tsunami wave. And I see this high breach-wall. And the wave is just hitting against this breach-wall and it is trying to get through, but it can't. And on the other side, I can see children playing, and I know one of them is you, even though it is not adult you. I see this child playing, and most of the kids can play. But you know what is on the other side of that wall and you have trouble just trusting in the protection of the breach-wall. But it doesn't matter how angry the wave, it doesn't matter how big the wave, that wall of protection is higher and thicker and stronger, and deeper. And I think that God has you in this place and He is surrounding you with others with childlike faith and He is recreating this childlike innocence and trust and freedom. Just like children playing with such freedom—they giggle and they laugh with delight; that's being restored in you ... this childlikeness, this innocence, and purity, and this simple trust that comes from that.

—Maryann Ward

I REMEMBER LYING AWAKE IN MY BED, TERRIFIED THAT SOMEONE WOULD COME IN AND SNATCH me. It had happened to a little girl in a nearby city. I had inadvertently heard about the incident on the radio. I was just little, but at that moment I understood that the world was not a safe place. Bad things happen to little ones, innocent ones. Someone can *get you* at any moment—something bad can happen to you anywhere, anytime. I was not safe. My innocence was gone and that sense of foreboding crept in to take its place. I had opened the door to fear, doubt, and intimidation, and it began to spread.

When fear and its companions come in, so does the belief in the lie that God cannot keep us safe. We doubt the power of God and the promise of His protection. This allows the enemy to gain access into our lives. Since we don't trust God to be able to keep us safe, we expect not to be safe (and thus give all the power to the enemy), and we don't feel safe. We do not feel protected because we don't believe we'll be protected. We refuse to believe the truth of God's Word, in essence, rejecting the Word of God and reinforcing the doubt and fear that has taken hold of our hearts. Fear, doubt, and intimidation reign in our lives, leaving no room for faith, hope, and assurance of God's loving protection.

As I grew a little older, I became more aware of the tragic events transpiring around the world, both natural and those of human initiative, making the fear and doubt in my life explode. Since I had a deeply sensitive and compassionate nature, this upset me to the point of being unbearable for my young heart. I remember the day I chose to shut down that part of me where sensitivity and compassion overflowed. It was a sad day, but I felt I had to do it—it hurt too much to feel the pain of others. I couldn't handle it. It was tearing my soul. I no longer wanted to know what was going on, nor feel what others were feeling. I didn't know what to do with it or about it. I was so little; I was completely overwhelmed.

What I didn't understand at the time was because of fear, I was choosing to walk away from the very gifting God had given me as a part of my role in the building of His Kingdom—compassion and caring for others: interceding for them and bearing their burdens. In doing so, I also allowed the enemy to come in with his opposite spirit. It was fascinating (and humbling) how this came to light so clearly one day at McDonald's during my prescribed season of identity.

I was standing in line and a critical thought about the person in front of me jumped into my head. My heart cried out, *Lord, why does this happen? This is not the way I think about people! This is not what I am about! This is not who I am, nor what I want to be! Why is this happening? I love people! In my heart, I want to help them, not critique them!*

The Lord's response was astoundingly clear: "The enemy is attacking your compassion."

I almost laughed out loud—the real-life version. It all suddenly made so much sense. My sister had once said how the look of compassion on my face as I ministered to others on the prayer line made her want to weep. Yet at other times, absolutely contrary thoughts would bombard my mind, encouraging me to criticize or judge others—usually in my head, but regretfully, sometimes out loud.

Understanding dawned. When I consciously made the decision (though young and unaware of the implications) to shut the door to God's gift of compassion, I had unknowingly opened the door to the spirit of criticism and judgment—its polar opposite. This put a target on my back, and the enemy was free to torment me with these spirits for many years—and so began the battle.

But praise God that He is the One who restores! Having already dealt with the fear and lies of God not being able to keep me safe, I slammed that ugly door shut and invited the flood of compassion that is at the core of who I am to be restored in the fulness God intended it to be. And I thanked Him that now, after all my years of training, I knew exactly what to do with it! It would become the gift it was meant to be. I ripped that enemy target right off of my back!

> Unravel more of who you are by looking at who you are not ... because that is more of who you were intended to be.

But it didn't stop there. God showed me that I could unravel more of who I was by looking at who I was *not* because that was more of who I was intended to be! He led me to reflect on all of the negative self-talk I have been guilty of speaking over myself all these years, and that which was spoken over me ... anything that began with "*I am* (plus a negative), *I don't, I can't, I am not* ... (*You are, you don't, you can't*...)" As the list tumbled out of my pen, I began to see patterns and connections. And as I compared my negative beliefs of who I currently was with my prophecies from the Lord, I was shocked with the revelation of how systematically the enemy had been attempting to dismantle every plan of the Lord for my life.

What had become many of my foundational beliefs of who I was … were all lies of the enemy—skillfully, strategically, and sadistically planted over the years in a desperate bid to keep me from being the person I was created to be. If the enemy could steal the very essence of who God designed me to *be*, I could therefore not *do* the very things I was designed to do.

The one who is to prophesy and release destiny over strangers has believed all of her life that she is shy—can't talk to strangers. The one who has deep wells of joy within, designed to be spread to others, doesn't laugh out loud, is dull, boring, and a waste of time to be with. The one who is to write books upon books has nothing of any value to say, has no voice … is invisible. She has been effectively silenced—until now.

As God healed and is healing my identity and I continue to come out of alignment with those lies as soon as they are discovered, I see more and more the ways in which I have not been walking in my identity based on the truth of who God says I am. Rather, I have been standing on the false foundation of lies built by the enemy. He has relentlessly attacked me in the area of my greatest giftings. He tried to steal my "princess." He tried to rob me of my intimate relationships. He tried to steal my countenance of joy, my compassion, my voice, my prophetic voice, and my destiny. But he has been exposed and now I know the truth of who I am. I can now begin to walk in the freedom, power, and authority God has given me as His daughter.

The sad part is, the one that drives me, is that the enemy still has a grip on so many people around the world, and is preventing them from knowing who they are and walking in the fulness of their destinies. He is stealing their very lives from them, as he tried to steal mine, and they don't even know it. And chances are, he is stealing so many things from *you*, and you don't even realize it—don't even see it. But smile, my friend. The time is *now* to be restored by the One and only King of kings. He knows *exactly* who you are and is excited to show you. All you have to do is ask!

Prophetic Word - May 2017

I can't remember what they call it with horses ... where they keep taking them through a drill with different kinds of scary scenarios so the horse will trust the owner and the owner will know the horse. It is that kind of process. God is leading you through all these scary kinds of things and every time He leads you through, the trust is building and you are getting to the place where ... "He is leading. I know I can trust Him. I'm going with Him." You wish He'd do it the same way all the time so you'll know it's Him, but no, He is walking you through this process where you can trust Him with this childlike innocence. Wherever He leads, wherever you go together, you know, you know, you know He's got your back, He's got your front, He is that wall of protection that you've always wanted, needed, and wished you had. He is there.

—MaryAnn Ward

Pushing Up

A. Unraveling the Threads

Unravel who you are by looking at who you are NOT because that is more of WHO YOU ARE! Understand that the enemy purposely and strategically attacks your greatest giftings, trying to prevent them from being activated and brought into fulness. Areas in which you struggle the most, and those which have been greatly under attack are key points of revelation. You are often designed to be the opposite of what you may have believed yourself to be for much of your life. Two foundational lies I had believed about myself were, "I'm too shy to talk to people," and "I have nothing to say." Had I continued to believe these lies, I would have been effectively shut down from some of the core purposes God had designed for my life.

What is your negative self-talk? Determining the negative beliefs you hold about yourself will start the deconstruction process of foundational lies controlling your life and holding you back from God's purposes. Negative self-talk will most likely begin with such words as:

I don't ... I can't ... I am not ... I will never/always ... I am (plus a negative).

Negative beliefs can also manifest as how you think others feel about you:

People don't/always ...

What has been spoken over you? It will usually sound like:

You don't ... You can't ... You are not ... You will never/always ... You are (plus a negative).

The lies you are believing may seem true in your experience, but it is not God's truth of who He designed you to be.

_____
_____
_____
_____

B. Connecting the Dots

Ask Holy Spirit to reveal the connections and patterns in the systematic attack of the enemy against you as he attempts to steal God's true design for you, and ultimately, your destiny. Ask Holy Spirit to help you break off the lies and understand the truth, God's truth, of who He created you to be.

To begin to see these patterns, sort the lies you have recorded on the previous pages by writing lies with similar themes into the same box, and giving the box a title that reflects what the enemy is trying to steal. For example, *"I am shy, I can't talk to strangers,* and *I can't pray for anyone outside of the church,"* would be written in one box and the title could read, "Stealing my Voice."

C. Breaking off Old Alignments

Pray to cast out the spirit of fear.

Prayer:

Fear, doubt, and intimidation, I will not tolerate you any longer! I bind you up! Enemy, take your minions and **GET OUT**! You are defeated! The Lord has not given me a spirit of fear, but of love, power, and a sound mind. Fear, doubt, and intimidation, I cast you out, in the mighty name of Jesus! I cancel all enemy attacks against the soundness of my mind. I revoke all efforts of the enemy to fill me with panic and dread. In the name of Jesus, I reverse all muscle memory that leads to Post Traumatic Stress Disorder, or any other mental disorder.

In Jesus' name, I take authority over all powers and principalities that are trying to keep me from trusting the Lord, and His power, and His authority in my life. Amen.

Read through each box from the previous pages and break off the lies that have been revealed, coming out of alignment with each one. Say the words out loud, confidently, and boldly. For example, the lie to break for the enemy trying to steal your voice is "I have no voice."

"I break off the lie that says I have no voice!"
If you believe people don't care about you, that is a lie against your worth or value.
"I come out of alignment with the lie that says I am not worth pursuing!"
"I come out of alignment with the lie that says I am not valuable!"

D. Forging New Alignments

Read back through each box of lies and write down God's truth, which is often the exact opposite of the lie, in the space provided below and on the next page. Continually ask Holy Spirit to show you His truth and wisdom for each one. Shout out each declaration!

"I come into agreement with God's truth that I have a voice! I am worth hearing! In fact, I have words upon words upon words that must be shared!"

"I come into agreement with God's truth that I am worthy in His sight! I am loved so much so that the King of kings died for me!"

E. Collecting Keys

Fear is a weapon of the enemy deliberately used to block your involvement with certain things, or to keep you from putting yourself in specific circumstances or situations. The things you fear, have an aversion to, or even strongly dislike are likely areas in which the Lord wants you to walk. You need to ask yourself, *"Why the fear? Why the aversion? What is the enemy so determined to keep me from, and why?"* <u>Understanding what the enemy is trying to prevent is the **key to unlocking you** and allowing you to walk in your full potential in that area.</u>

For a time in my life I was deathly afraid of knives. I was sure that a butcher knife would eventually become a part of my demise. Horrible thoughts would flash across my mind each time I picked one up. I wanted to lock them all away before I went to bed at night. I now do warfare with a dagger, much like others do with flags and banners—not a huge stretch to understanding why the enemy tried so desperately to keep me from all things sharp!!

At times, knowing the entrance wound of the fear is necessary, and the Lord will thus reveal it. Other times, the wound can be cleansed and healed without even knowing how it was originally inflicted.

On the following pages, list your fears and strong dislikes. Ask Holy Spirit to reveal any necessary keys. Ask for revelation for where the fear originated, but do not be concerned if it is not revealed. You may have to add to this list over time as the fears and keys are revealed to you. **Pray to cut off the fear, close the entrance point (heal the wound) and open the new door of opportunity with each new revelation.**

"I cut off the fear of ...
I close the entrance point and ask You to heal and seal the wound. Lord, please open the door of ...
(whatever the fear was blocking you from doing)."

> Key - Understanding what the enemy is trying to hold you back from being or doing by giving you the fear

Fear/Aversion: Key:

Fear/Aversion: Key:

Fear/Aversion: Key

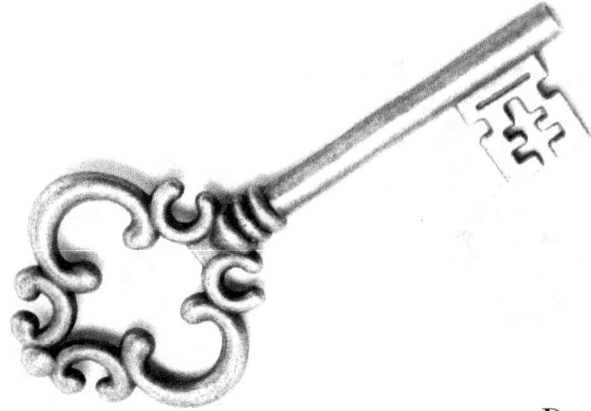

Fear/Aversion: Key

Pray to cut off each fear and seal the wound. Pray to open each new door of opportunity the Lord has for you with the key!!! Be brave!

F. Turning it Over to the Lord

The root of fear, doubt, and intimidation, no matter the entrance wound, concludes with us *not trusting God* to keep us and our loved ones safe and protected, to heal us, to restore us, to provide for us, to honor us in His timing, to love us, to speak to us, to teach us, to show us our path …

It is time to bring this mistrust before the Lord in repentance, and watch what He will do!

> Blessed is the one whose transgression is forgiven, whose sin is covered.
> I will instruct you and teach you in the way you should go; I will counsel you with my eye upon you. Be not like a horse or a mule, without understanding, which must be curbed with bit and bridle, or it will not stay near you. Many are the sorrows of the wicked, but steadfast love surrounds the one who trusts in the LORD.
> **Psalm 32:1, 8-10**

Prayer:

Dear Lord, I have been walking in my own ways instead of Your ways. I have not trusted You with some of the things closest to my heart. I repent for:

_____
_____
_____
_____
_____
_____
_____
_____

Prayer continued:

As a part of walking in my own ways, I have put safeguards and behaviors in my life to try to cover those areas in which I have not been trusting You. They are not a part of Your plan for me, but rather, they are keeping me from walking in the fulness of my salvation and my destiny. Holy Spirit, please reveal these safeguards and behaviors I have inadvertently installed that are not of You. **(Record any revelations, both pictures, and words.)**

I release each one of these safeguards and behaviors to You. I give You permission to fully destroy them. Do what it takes, Lord, to set me free from captivity of these very things, and allow You to work fully in my life, as I fully trust You with *all* things. Grow my trust, O Lord! Build my faith!

G. Fighting Back

It is time to fight back and recover your lost territory. Much can be stolen as fear has pushed in over the years of our lives.

What have you lost because of the systematic attack of fear?

_____
_____
_____
_____
_____
_____
_____

(Give yourself time to grieve over your losses as the sadness surfaces.)

Prayer:

    Holy Spirit, please release Your power, joy, faith, love, peace, and hope over my life. Help me to increase my faith and build my trust in the Lord, who will lift me up with His powerful right hand. He will rescue me in my time of need. He will provide for me. He will honor me as I humble myself before Him. He will restore me. He will teach me and guide me. He loves me and I will trust in Him!

    I take back… (list the things you have lost, as listed above.)

I ask You to restore any giftings I have suppressed. I willingly open the door to them so I can be a part of building Your Kingdom, for Your glory. I cast down my crown at Your feet, and ask that all circumstances of my giftings be used in Your way, for Your glory alone. I ask for boldness to step out and do everything You ask me to do with everything You have bestowed upon me. Open them up! I give them to You. I lay them at Your feet. I pray this in Jesus' name, amen.

H. Forging a New Path

What will your life now be like without fear holding you back? What are you going to do differently? What God-given hopes and dreams have you not followed because of fear, doubt or intimidation? What God-directed risks has fear held you back from taking?

_____
_____
_____
_____
_____
_____
_____
_____
_____
_____
_____
_____

Write a decree to put this new knowledge into practice from this moment forward!

"I will …

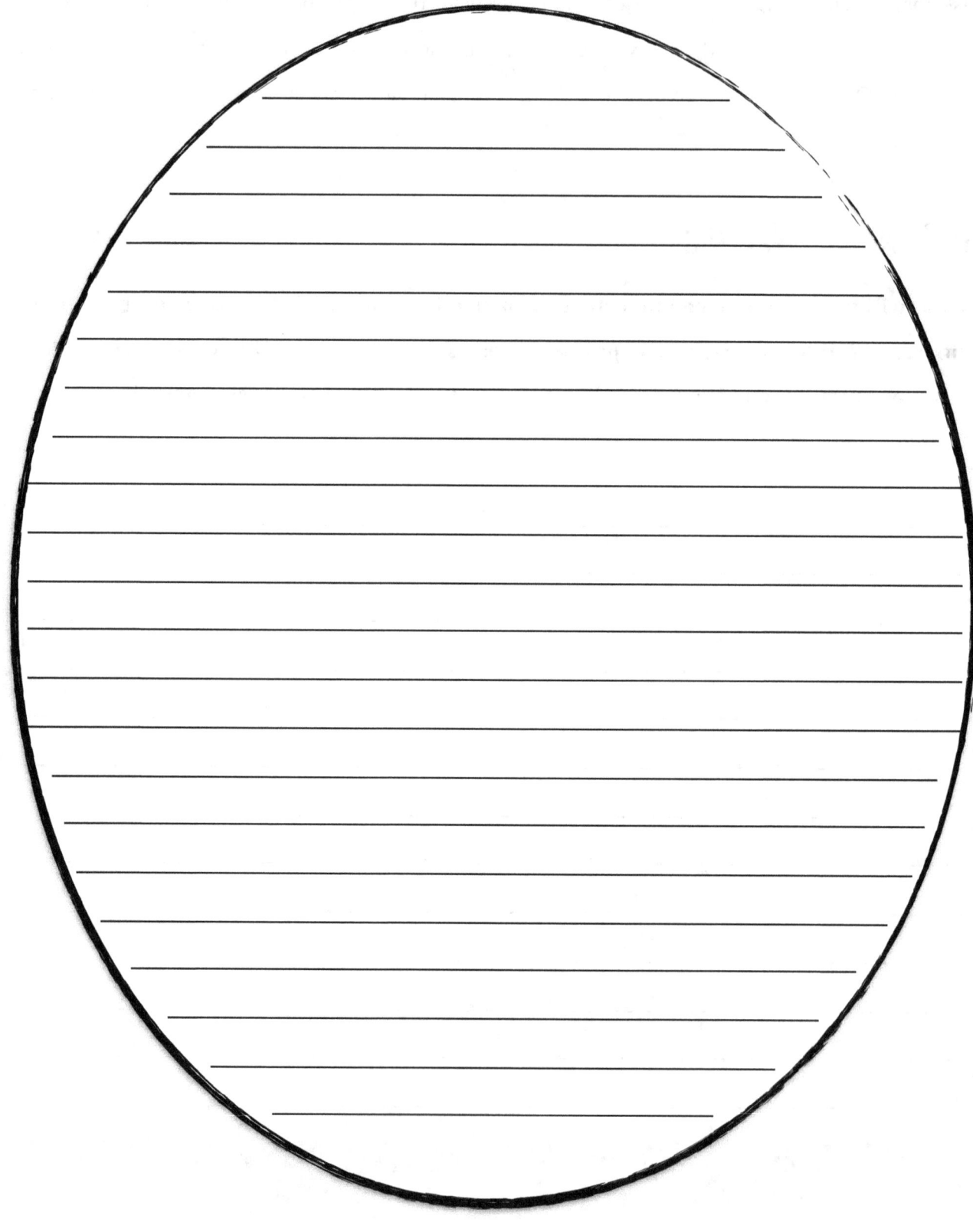

I. Stepping into Battle

As you step out of fear, doubt, and intimidation, the Lord is eagerly waiting on the other side, ready to anoint you, make covenants with you, and to hand you your new assignments that lead into the fulfillment of your destiny.

Spend some quiet time before the Lord, with your crown surrendered at His feet, asking Him to speak to your heart in this regard.

As you receive a sense of your anointing, assignments, and covenants, remember, He is faithful in giving you confirmation through His Word and through others. This is a process and will happen over the course of days, or even months. As He brings these revelations to you, continue to record them to preserve the voice of the Lord speaking in your life.

His Truth

Speak the truth of God's Word as you step into new life.

Those who live in the shelter of the Most High will find rest in the shadow of the Almighty.

This I declare about the LORD: He alone is my refuge, my place of safety; he is my God, and I trust him.

For he will rescue you from every trap and protect you from deadly disease.

He will cover you with his feathers. He will shelter you with his wings.

His faithful promises are your armor and protection.

Do not be afraid of the terrors of the night, nor the arrow that flies in the day.

Do not dread the disease that stalks in darkness, nor the disaster that strikes at midday.

Though a thousand fall at your side, though ten thousand are dying around you, these evils will not touch you.

Just open your eyes, and see how the wicked are punished.

If you make the LORD your refuge, if you make the Most High your shelter, no evil will conquer you; no plague will come near your home.

For he will order his angels to protect you wherever you go.

They will hold you up with their hands so you won't even hurt your foot on a stone.

You will trample upon lions and cobras; you will crush fierce lions and serpents under your feet!

The LORD says, "I will rescue those who love me. I will protect those who trust in my name.

When they call on me, I will answer; I will be with them in trouble.

I will rescue and honor them. I will reward them with a long life and give them my salvation."

Psalm 91 (NLT)

Declaring His Truth

Declare His promises in Psalm 91 boldly and with faith.

> I find rest in the shadow of the Almighty.
>
> The Lord alone is my refuge, my place of safety.
>
> The Lord is my God, and I trust Him.
>
> He rescues me from every trap.
>
> He protects me from disease.
>
> He covers me with His feathers.
>
> He shelters me with His wings.
>
> His faithful promises are my armor and protection.
>
> I am not afraid of the terrors of the night, nor the arrow that flies in the day.
>
> I do not dread the disease that stalks in darkness,
>
> nor the disaster that strikes at midday.
>
> Evil does not touch me.
>
> Evil does not conquer me; no plague will come near my home.
>
> He orders His angels to protect me wherever I go.
>
> They will hold me up with their hands so I won't even hurt my foot on a stone.
>
> I trample upon lions and cobras; I crush fierce lions and serpents under my feet!
>
> I trust in His name. When I call on Him, He answers; He is with me in trouble.
>
> He rescues and honors me.
>
> He rewards me with a long life and He gives me His salvation.

Unit Four

Expectancy

"How come you don't access the resources available to you?"

I left the counselor's office deeply pondering her question. *Yes, why did I find it so very difficult to ask for help?* I could ask my family when I needed to do so. They are my heroes, always doing more than the expected for me, filling in the gaps during my many difficult times. Often, I wouldn't even have to ask—they'd see a need and just step in. It was outside of that I *could not, would not* ask for help, until I became absolutely desperate. But when I did finally ask, I would not seem to get the help I needed, or I'd even receive the exact opposite.

But we get what we expect. Our beliefs about ourselves and our situations direct our decisions and thus our actions. This impacts others' beliefs, and therefore their behaviors and actions toward us. In psychology, this is known as a self-fulfilling prophecy. And this, the Lord told me, was another mountain in my life we had to move.

And yes, many, many of my life situations seemed to prove that very thing. I had received exactly what I had expected to receive—the *opposite* of what I felt I needed. The recent issue involved praying for more time and finances … and a situation immediately occurred that resulted in a reduction of the very things for which I had asked.

With even my prayer life being assaulted, I knew it was time to dig deep to find out what I was believing in my heart that gave permission for this phenomenon to repeatedly occur. For as I believed in my heart, so was I (Proverbs 23:7).

As I sifted through the dirt which buried me, I could see it was a stronghold in my life—a system of lies holding a false belief in place. To move this internal mountain (thank you, Kimm, for your perspective on internal mountains), I had to keep chipping away at it, revealing layer upon layer of lies, repenting and coming out of alignment with them, until the core belief at its center could be exposed. From there, I could ask the Lord for His truth.

In the midst of the excavation process, I asked God to reveal the key incident that planted the lie, "I will always receive the opposite of what I ask." He immediately brought to mind what seemed like an insignificant disappointment I had faced in grade seven or eight. For my birthday that year, I had asked for an Adidas gym-bag, any color except yellow and black, and a piece of jewelry, anything except for a bracelet. And you guessed it—I received a yellow and black gym-bag and a bracelet.

It was not heartbreaking or any such thing at the time. I remember quickly shrugging it off and enjoying them anyway. However, it is interesting to note that the enemy can plant lies in even the most subtle of ways and circumstances. We sometimes think we have to always look to the big events of death, loss, trauma, and disaster to find enemy lies when in reality, many of the more devious lies are planted in the simplest of manners. This can make them even more treacherous, as they are more difficult to find—for they are hidden in plain sight. We sometimes even talk ourselves out of the impact they have had on our lives, thinking, *How can such a tiny seed have turned into such a devastating root?*

This event and other such ones led to a network of lies that had built up a structure, or belief system, in my life under which I functioned and upon which I based my decisions and actions. And this false belief system was also the foundation on which I determined the **expectations** for my life. When it was all laid out on paper as God led me through the steps of my healing, I could sadly see I had more negative expectations for my life than positive ones.

> We may not receive what we want in life, but we often receive exactly what we expect to receive.

My life, at this point, had not been the picture perfect one I'd hoped for, and certainly not what I had been dreaming about. But as I looked over all the lies I had held at the core of my belief system for so many years, what I had been aligning myself with, I realized I did not receive what I wanted, but I did get much of what I had expected. Some of the deceptions I lived by were:

- ✗ I will receive the opposite of what I ask for.
- ✗ I will lose everyone I get close to.
- ✗ Who am I that people should go out of their way for me?
- ✗ I am not worth pursuing.
- ✗ Everything will eventually go wrong.
- ✗ My needs will not be met.
- ✗ Deep down, people don't care about me.
- ✗ I am being selfish and weak if I ask for help.
- ✗ I will never have what I truly want.
- ✗ People will treat me poorly and I have to accept it if I want relationships.
- ✗ I have to do everything myself.
- ✗ I will never live in peace or joy.
- ✗ I will never be truly free.

This was an ugly picture, and not what I wanted for my life any longer. I chose to instead align with the truth of His Word in Ephesians 3:20: "Now to him who is able to do exceedingly abundantly above all that we ask or think, according to the power that works in us …" (NKJV).

> As you get hit with wave upon wave of nasty stuff, you either break or quit or numb—or rise up.

I was faced with a lot of negative to overcome, but with the Lord's guidance, I knew it was possible. That's the intriguing aspect in the process of being brought to the point of breaking over and over again, as had been my journey over these past many years. As you get hit with wave upon wave of nasty stuff, you either break or quit or numb—or rise up. I had learned to rise up and keep fighting for my complete healing and freedom. It's a brutal process, but very effective!

Lord, I thought I was done my healing. Haven't I been through enough? But God knew otherwise. He wanted to take me even deeper. And that meant even more refining. And this time it would perhaps hurt even more. It did. It does. But it was and is worth it.

Prophetic word - March 2017 (abridged)

At one time you were clay and Jesus was the potter. He took that clump of shapeless clay and formed and fashioned it into a clay pot, or something beautiful. But then I feel like there has been a bit of a transition. Now it is almost like you are this absolutely valuable piece of marble. Jesus is still the artisan, but it is not the same as when it was clay. It is now more difficult because it is now chipping and hammering and a lot of cutting away, but the result is so much more beautiful.

A clay pot is beautiful, but a marble statue is this incredible work of art. I feel that even though there has been more pain associated with this process, you can also testify to how the fruit is so, so great. A clay pot is easier to break; there is much more fragility. God has made you strong. It is pretty hard to break a big piece of marble. I think there is a real strengthening that has come. God has brought a lot of fortification into you. There has been a real hardness of will and resolve to follow the Lord. You are becoming this stunning work of art that He is delighting in. He looks at you and is thrilled with the work that is being done. Just continue to trust in Him, even through these difficult chipping away times, because you know that He has the end product in mind, He sees the finished work ... the artist can see, and that is good.

—Tanya Foster

When I finally broke through, the almost imperceptible hidden lie was, *God won't meet my needs.* As a Christian, when you don't believe this most basic tenant, you develop an independent, self-reliant mentality. This mentality told me, "I can do it myself," because I believed I had to do it myself. And whether you are around people a lot or not, this false belief puts you into a form of isolation, rather than in the community God has ordained.

The fact I lived alone much of my life, or alone with my kids, (even when I was married I had to do most things on my own), led to a hardening of my heart, reinforcing this independent spirit. I felt I had to harden myself to survive. I often told myself, "I'm strong, I'm tough. I don't need anyone. I can take care of myself." I would put my head up or down, depending on the situation, and pretend I didn't care, it didn't matter, it was fine. So many times I said, "It was fine —I was fine," to myself and others when inside, my heart was breaking. Eventually, you become numb to it and it becomes a way of life. You forget others can help you. You forget God is there to work things out in ways you cannot even fathom, if you only ask, believe, and trust. You figure out creative ways to do everything by yourself, for yourself. You busily spend all of your time taking care of everyone and everything else, putting yourself on the bottom of the priority pile, over and over again until something snaps. And it is usually you.

When we don't trust God to meet our needs, and if we are not in a place to do it ourselves, we also put unjustified and unrealistic expectations on other people, expecting them to fulfill needs that really aren't theirs to fulfill. Though God will often use people to meet our needs, it has to be in His ways and in His timing, and that will most likely be different than how we think it should be done.

Therefore, we need to release people from all expectations to meet our needs and trust God to do so. And trusting God to meet our needs means understanding the difference between our *needs* and our *wants*. He may not meet all our *wants*, but He will meet our *needs* as He sees them, in a manner that will form and fashion us into who He needs us to be for the bigger purpose of His will for our life. As Romans 8:28 says, "And we know that all things work together for good to those who love God, to those who are called according to *His* purpose" (NKJV). Sometimes we forget about the "according to His purpose" part. And this means **surrendering our will to Him.**

This means dying to our own lives, our flesh; dying to the way we wanted our life to unfold, and picking up the cross. But in doing so, we need to realize that He has specifically designed us for a purpose in this life, and when we are fully walking as who we truly are, doing what He has created us to do, it is then that we will find pure joy. He sees the bigger picture of our life, knows all the pieces and how they fit together. We only see with limited vision, the pieces right in front of us. He knows where we are going, and how He needs to get us there. This makes it exceedingly worthwhile to trust that He will meet our needs … even if it is uncomfortable … even if it hurts.

Pushing Up

A. Revealing Targets

It is difficult to receive God's promises for our lives when we carry negative expectations, as our expectations are often met.

What are the *brutally honest* negative expectations for your life that you carry deep in your heart? Pray for Holy Spirit revelation.

B. Walking in Repentance

Often, our negative expectations stem from a deep-seated mistrust in God being able to meet our needs. God's Word explicitly says, "And my God will supply every need of yours according to his riches in glory in Christ Jesus" (Philippians 4:19). This is the truth. As we align with anything outside of this truth, we become self-reliant, and therefore, limited to only the resources we can supply ourselves. As we realign with God's truth, we step into the miraculous. Realignment begins with the gift of repentance.

Which of your negative expectations are based on *not trusting God*? Confess and repent for *not trusting God* to meet your needs. (Continue to repent for any situations revealed throughout this unit where your responses to negative expectations have led to sin.) Ask Holy Spirit for this revelation.

"I repent for not trusting You, Lord, with/for …"

"I repent of …"

_____
_____
_____
_____
_____
_____
_____
_____

Declare: "Lord, I realign with Your truth: You will meet all my needs!"

C. Removing Targets

Ask the Lord to show you which negative expectation statements from the "Revealing Targets" section are lies contrary to His Word, which you have been deceived into believing and aligning yourself with. Highlight the ones He shows you. Ask Him to reveal the truth of His Word in each situation. Break off each highlighted lie and realign yourself with God's truth for each one by speaking the opposite. They may overlap with the lies that led to you not trusting God.

Prayer:

Dear Lord, as I have walked through the disappointments in my life I seem to have pocketed the many negative things that have happened to me. They have since ganged up and taken over some areas of my life, leading me to hold a depressive countenance. I have come to expect negative circumstances rather than the promises of a good Father. Lies of negativity have been planted in my heart and I have unknowingly been empowering them. This makes for an ugly picture—one that I will no longer accept. You are able to do exceedingly abundantly above all I ask or think, and that belief is what I choose to empower.

I break off the lie _____.

God's truth is _____.

(Repeat with each highlighted lie.)

On the following page, write out the expectations you should hold in your heart, as declared above—the ones that align with the truth of God's Word. Read them over in declaration until they fully settle into your soul. Add any Scriptures that comes to your mind.

D. Letting Go

Sometimes when we are not trusting God to meet our needs, we put expectations on other people to meet them. Though God often uses people to meet our needs, it is not for us to expect them to do so, especially on our own terms. When people do not meet these needs, we can unjustly hold an offense against them.

Look back over your list of negative expectations for your life to determine if some of them stem from placing unwarranted expectations on others or on yourself. Write a prayer to forgive and release any people on whom you have misplaced expectations, letting them "off the hook" of expectation. Include yourself, others, and God (when you have dictated how and when He should meet your needs).

_____
_____
_____
_____
_____
_____
_____
_____
_____
_____
_____
_____
_____

Is there anyone from whom you need to ask for forgiveness?

E. Realigning Inner Vows

Ask Holy Spirit to reveal any inner vows you have made in association with each of the lies you have believed. Refer back to your revealed targets to guide you. Remember, vows often begin with the words "*I will never/always…*"

Cancel the agreement you had made through the vow, then record and declare its opposite.

F. Breaking Free

Ask Holy Spirit to reveal to you if you have been operating under any spirits such as a spirit of independence, pride, rebellion, stubbornness, jealousy, despair, etc. Take time to listen to His voice. If any are revealed, break them off.

Prayer:

Dear Lord, I repent of partnering with the spirit of _____.
I cast out this spirit, in the name of Jesus, and send it to the foot of the cross. I will not partner with it any longer. It no longer will be a part of my life.

G. Practicing Gratitude

The Lord loves a grateful heart. It can mean the difference between receiving all He has for you and rejecting His love and His plans for you. It is difficult to accept the love of God if you don't trust Him to meet your needs … as you have a need for love!

Write a prayer thanking the Lord for how He has been loving you and meeting your needs and those of your loved ones throughout the past many years.

_____
_____
_____
_____
_____
_____
_____

H. Walking in Surrender

Write a prayer *surrendering your will* to God, submitting yourself to trust Him to meet your needs and to guide your life in the way He has designed to form and fashion you into who you need to be for His bigger purposes.

_____
_____
_____
_____
_____
_____
_____
_____

I. Praying into Your Unmet Needs

Pray with a partner, asking God to meet those needs you feel are unmet and to reveal any blocks that are preventing them from being met.

_____
_____
_____
_____
_____
_____
_____
_____

J. Listening to the Lord

Ask the Lord to show you a picture or give you a word or a Scripture to plant His seeds of truth in your heart of His promise to you in an area of unmet needs. Ask the Lord to show you how He sees you, how He loves you, how He is meeting and will meet your needs according to His glorious riches.

His Truth

Speak the truth of His provision as you submit to Him and walk as He calls you.

Now to him who is able to do far more abundantly than all we ask or think according to the power at work within …
Ephesians 3:20

For the LORD God is a sun and shield; the LORD bestows favor and honor. No good thing does he withhold from those who walk uprightly.
Psalm 84:11

"Ask, and it will be given to you; seek, and you will find; knock, and it will be opened to you. For everyone who asks receives, and the one who seeks finds, and to the one who knocks it will be opened.
Matthew 7:7-8

And God is able to make all grace abound to you, so that having all sufficiency in all things at all times, you may abound in every good word. As it is written, "He has distributed freely, he has given to the poor; his righteousness endures forever." He who supplies seed to the sower and bread for food will supply and multiply your seed for sowing and increase the harvest of your righteousness.
2 Corinthians 9:8-10

The eyes of all look to you, and you give them their food in due season. You open your hand; you satisfy the desire of every living thing.
Psalm 145:15-16

For he satisfies the longing soul, and the hungry soul he fills with good things.
Psalm 107:9

If this be so, our God whom we serve is able to deliver us from the burning fiery furnace, and he will deliver us out of your hand, O king.
Daniel 3:17

I am the LORD your God, who brought you up out of the land of Egypt. Open your mouth wide, and I will fill it. "But my people did not listen to my voice; Israel would not submit to me.
Psalm 81:10-11

Then Jesus told his disciples, "If anyone would come after me, let him deny himself and take up his cross and follow me. For whoever would save his life will lose it, but whoever loses his life for my sake will find it.
Matthew 16:24-25

I have been crucified with Christ. It is no longer I who live, but Christ who lives in me.
And the life I now live in the flesh I live by faith in the Son of God,
who loved me and gave himself for me.

Praying His Truth

Lord God, You are the Alpha and the Omega, the Beginning and the End, who is and was and who is to come. You are able to do far more abundantly than all I ask or imagine, through Your power at work within me. Thank You for being my sun and shield, giving me grace and glory. Thank You that as I walk in Your righteousness, You bring favor and honor to my life; You grant me all I need, withholding no good thing. Help me to continually do what is right in Your eyes. Thank You that as I ask, seek, and knock, You heed my call and generously provide all I need with much left over to share with others. Thank You for providing increase in my resources and producing a great harvest through me as I am obedient to You. Lord God, open Your hand and satisfy the godly desires that flood my soul as I look to You in hope. Satisfy my longing, hungry soul, O Lord! I hunger and thirst for You! Thank You for filling me with good things! I ask for the food I need, at the times You determine I need it. Deliver me from every fiery furnace I am facing Lord, as I learn to walk in Your presence more and more. I open my mouth wide and wait in expectant hope for You to fill it, as I continue to submit my soul to You. Help me to lay everything down at Your altar, O Lord, even those things which my heart fights so hard to keep a tight hold on. Help me deny myself more and more, as I pick up my cross and faithfully follow You. Let me gain my life by losing it, for Your glory. I hold myself up to be crucified with You, Jesus. It is no longer I who live, but You who lives in me. Help me to live by faith in You, Lord Jesus, as You have given Yourself up for me because of Your love for me.

Unit Five

Treasure Hunt

Pray the Truth of God's Word to lead you into all He has for you.

SITTING AT MY KITCHEN TABLE THAT DAY WAITING … I CAN IMAGINE THE EXCITEMENT I MUST have felt. *He* was coming to see *me*! I had cleaned my house, weeded my garden (I hated weeding), prepared the meal … I had made sure everything was *perfect*.

Waiting … waiting … as the minutes and then hours passed, I can only imagine how anxious I must have felt when he had not arrived, yet had not contacted me. The drive was not that long—he should have arrived long ago. Perhaps I was verging on *frantic* by the time I started trying to contact him, then people who knew him. As it was the pre-cellphone era, I pictured him stranded somewhere on the highway, unable to contact me. Or, God forbid, he was perhaps in an accident, trapped under the weight of the overturned vehicle.

I believed I contacted the hospitals, hoping it was an overdramatic response to my fear at his absence. And I cannot even imagine what my sense of helplessness would have been as I went to sleep that night—if I even slept at all.

You may have noticed all of my reactions are suppositions—I have almost no memory of this event. It was recounted to me in detail recently, by my good friend who would have known those things about my life during that time period. And she would have been the one to pick up the pieces. But as she spoke, flashes of it blinked through my mind and heart, and it absolutely fit the pattern of what was to be our relationship over the next too many years.

I would find out the next day he was fine; he just had decided not to come (if he ever even had the intention of coming). For me to explain why he had not bothered to call instead of allowing me to become frantic with worry would be pure conjecture on my part, as he never did. But I would soon learn this very pattern of our relationship: absent communication no matter what the stakes—intentional or otherwise. I would attend all his functions and events, but trek to mine solo, or end up on my own after intentional sabotage. I would invest in all the particulars of his life—mine outside of his somehow did not seem to even exist.

But it was at that event, the Lord recently revealed to me, that the little lies of hopelessness deviously slipped into my chest and tried to steal my future. I believed, *Nothing I did mattered. Nothing would ever change. Nothing would ever work out; even the things that started well would end badly. I would always end up disappointed and hurt.* And so, with a heavy heart, I took a shovel and buried all of my hopes and dreams. And to seal it, I shoved this memory far back into the deep recesses of my mind, only to be retrieved so very many years later.

At the time, I didn't understand why I wasn't able to just walk away from the damaging relationship before I became so deeply entrenched. Why did I tolerate such poor treatment from another? People who knew me at the time were direct and honest about what they saw already happening, but I chose not to listen. After asking myself this same question for so many years, it has only been as God healed my identity that the reason was uncovered.

When you have believed, deep in your very being for so long, that the *boy* you like will never like you, you are a freak, you are not worth pursuing … (you get the picture)—it doesn't allow for any hope in a healthy relationship or in a future. It sets you up to accept the unacceptable, for you truly believe it will never be any different; cannot even be different. You thus begin to compromise, rationalize, and justify. You begin to lose who you are. So as the unconscious choice was made to surrender my soul, all hope unknowingly given up, despair taking over, what is one to do but bury all the treasures, all the gifts, all the dreams of one's heart, lock it, seal it, and forget who you are.

As disappointment, hurt, bitterness, and their ugly accomplices take root in our lives and grow, they slowly crowd out the promises of God. We cannot contain both. Regretfully, it is these promises, these treasures, these hopes and dreams that get dropped, lost along the path, and covered over.

But as God healed my identity, and layer upon layer of lies were released, I found these ones tucked so far beneath, and stepping out of alignment with them, was able to excavate the treasure chest God has for my life. "Hope deferred makes the heart sick …" (Proverbs 13:12). Hope restored … changes everything.

Pushing Up

A. Walking in Repentance

We have often already begun to compromise, rationalize, and justify before we hit our rock bottom and give up on the promises of God. **Confession of these things is a good starting point before we go on our treasure hunt!**

Prayer:

Oh Lord, thank You that You are so willing to hear my heart, no matter what is in it. As the disappointments began to mount in my life, Lord, and circumstances did not go my way, I chose to follow my own path instead of grasping tightly to Yours. I now choose to give You my disappointment, my hurt, my pain for You to heal. I cast down any bitterness I am carrying in my heart because of the disappointment and negative circumstances I have faced in my life. I repent for surrendering my soul to deception instead of tenaciously holding tight to Your promises. Help me to be steadfast and unwavering. Plant in me a backbone of titanium, and a face of flint.

Every place where my actions, thoughts, behaviors, and choices have been ungodly as I began to compromise, rationalize, and justify, Lord, please forgive me. I have not walked in a manner worthy of You. This is not the path You have chosen for my life. Holy Spirit, if there are any specific things for which I need to repent, please bring them to remembrance so I can realign myself with You and Your promises. (Give time for Holy Spirit revelation, then respond to His prompting. Record any revelations and needed responses.)

_____
_____
_____
_____
_____

B. Digging Deep

We often start along a new path to explore the promises of God with exhilaration and enthusiasm. But the journey can get long and the path can stretch out endlessly—far beyond our vision. Our hopes and dreams can slowly become clouded with the dust at our feet, or buried suddenly and violently with a landslide. Or, we may even choose to stop at the side of the road and bury them ourselves when the lies we are believing become too much for us, leading us into discouragement, despair, and hopelessness.

The lies may sound like:
- *Nothing I do matters.*
- *I don't make a difference.*
- *Nothing will ever change.*
- *I will always be disappointed or hurt.*
- *I'm not good at anything.*
- *I can't do that.*
- *That is impossible.*
- *I'll never make it.*
- *I'm being unrealistic/impractical.*
- *That's too big for me.*
- *I am hopeless.*
- *Things do not work out for me.*
- *Things start well but deteriorate.*
- *There is no point.*
- *I have no purpose.*
- *I am not capable.*
- *It will never work.*
- *Get your head out of the clouds.*
- *I'm not good enough.*
- *It's too hard.*
- *That situation is hopeless.*
- _____

Highlight any lies that seem familiar to your spirit. Add any that are trying to be heard.

Whether your hopes and dreams and your belief in the promises of God were buried intentionally or unconsciously, gradually or with a single event, they can be unearthed.

Pray for God to reveal how you lost hold of His promises for your life—your hopes and dreams—but know that it is not always necessary to know where, when, or how you lost them or let go of them for God to restore them! Record any revelations.

Prayer:

Dear Father God, I am ready to do the needed excavation of my heart. Holy Spirit, please show me what has happened to me that has led to the burial of hopes and dreams, known or unknown, in my life. Father, I trust You on this journey. I trust You with any pain as any forgotten memories are exposed. But if this is a time when I do not need to know how or when I was wounded, please just expose any lies of which I am still unaware. Show me Your truth about Your promises for my life and help me to realign with them. Resurrect the lost hopes and dreams and make them explode out of my heart and into the earthly realm with Your mighty power.

C. Recalibrating

Pray for healing of memories, wounds, and trauma. Come out of alignment with any exposed hope-stealing lies, and realign with God's truth. Use the sample prayer, or pray what Holy Spirit leads you to pray.

Prayer:

Dear Lord, my God,

Thank You for showing me _____.

Please heal every part of my heart that was traumatized and wounded at this time. Please show me where You were while this was happening; how You helped me through it, and how You are going to turn it around for the good. I come out of agreement with the lie(s):

_____
_____
_____

This is not Your truth for my life. Your truth is:

_____
_____
_____

Lord, I forgive:

_____
_____
_____

(Do you need to grieve any losses? Ask someone for forgiveness? Practice gratefulness?)

D. "X" marks the spot

What are the God-given hopes, dreams, and visions you carry? What lost parts of yourself need to be restored? **Write them! Sketch them! Pray them! Speak them out!**

Prayer Declaration:

Lord, I reclaim Your promises! I reclaim the hopes and dreams and visions for my life You have placed in my heart! I reclaim the godly desires of my heart! I reclaim all of the forgotten and lost parts of myself! Restore to my memory exactly who I am—exactly who You created me to be!

My Hopes & Dreams

E. Buried Treasure

Remind me of who You created me to be, Lord. How do you see me?

Heavenly Father, You have given me these talents, skills, abilities, character qualities, passions, and strengths:

His Truth

Let the restorative power of His Word of hope seep into the depths of your heart.

Let us hold fast the confession of our hope without

wavering, for he who promised is faithful.

Hebrews 10:23

And not only *that*, but we also glory in tribulations, knowing that tribulation produces

perseverance; and perseverance, character;

and character, hope. Now hope does not disappoint,

because the love of God has been poured out in our hearts

by the Holy Spirit who was given to us.

Romans 5:3-5 (NKJV)

May the God of hope fill you with all joy and peace in believing, so that by the power of

the Holy Spirit you may abound in hope.

Romans 15:13

I will restore the fortunes of my people Israel, and they shall rebuild the ruined cities and

inhabit them; they shall plant vineyards and drink their wine,

and they shall make gardens and eat their fruit.

Amos 9:14

Return to your stronghold, O prisoners of hope;
today I declare that I will restore to you double.
Zechariah 9:12

Do not neglect the gift you have, which was given you by prophecy when the council of elders laid their hands on you. Practice these things, immerse yourself in them,
so that all may see your progress.
1 Timothy 4:14-15

His lord said to him, 'Well *done*, good and faithful servant; you have been faithful over a few things, I will make you ruler over many things. Enter into the joy of your lord.'
Matthew 25:23 (NKJV)

For this reason I remind you to fan into flame the gift of God, which is in you through the laying on of my hands, for God gave us a spirit not of fear but of power and love and self-control.
2 Timothy 1:6-7

Declaring His Truth

Stand strong as you boldly proclaim all He has for you. Add your own proclamations.

> The Lord is the First and the Last. It is He who lives and was dead and is alive forevermore. I will hold fast to the confession of my hope without wavering, for He who promised is faithful. I will glory in my tribulations, knowing that tribulation produces perseverance; and perseverance, character; and character, hope. I trust in the hope of the Lord; hope does not disappoint because the love of God has been poured out in my heart Holy Spirit who was given to me. The God of hope will fill me with all joy. The God of hope will fill me with peace. I will abound in hope by the power of Holy Spirit. The Lord will restore my fortune and I shall rebuild every city the Lord calls me to rebuild.
>
> I will enjoy the fruit of my labor.
>
> The Lord will restore to me double for all that has been stolen from me. I will develop and practice the gifts and talents the Lord has given to me. I will immerse myself in them and learn all I can about them. I will fan them into flame and use them to their full extent and purpose, for the Lord has not given me a spirit of fear, but of power, love, and self-control. I will be faithful to my Lord.

Unit Six

The Question of Sexuality

Walking around my neighborhood with a trusted friend, I was recounting an inaccurate but oddly reoccurring theme in my life. As I stated the words, "It is almost as if the world is trying to set me up to believe I should be gay," the veil came off and revelation took hold. *It is.*

By my early twenties, though I had many male friendships and boyfriends beginning in grade six, I had not had a serious enough long-term relationship that warranted bringing them home for the dreaded *meet-the-extended-family* occasion. This factor, I can only assume, led my grandmother to inquire if it was *perhaps because I liked girls instead?*

And I do like girls—but not in the sexual way the world adamantly tries to promote. God has always graciously provided me with amazing female friends with whom I have had a strong bond. And most of these were healthy relationships with appropriate boundaries, though a few at different points of my life swayed toward co-dependency, though not in a sexual manner. We had fun spending time together, cared deeply about each other, and shared the level of intimacy common in close friends of the heart.

Even as a young girl I remember idolizing some of the older girls at school, wanting to be like them, noticed by them. But in today's hyper-sexualized society, the message is you cannot like someone without it being sexual. Society has warped the natural, same-sex intimacy intended for friendships into the sexualized version: same-sex attraction.

Attraction in itself is intended to be predominantly a social sorting process. I see this attraction continually functioning in most people's lives. In fact, it often dictates our social lives more than we realize, sorting such things as *couple friends* from those you can only spend individual time with because your spouse doesn't like their spouse! It is how we naturally choose those inner circle people; the ones we know we want to invest the time and effort it takes to establish and maintain a close friend. It is what takes those *certain ones* out of the realm of *acquaintance* and squeezes them into our hearts in a way that has them standing shoulder to shoulder with us on the front lines of our lives in one way or another. This can be a part of our daily walk, or for the ones geographically distanced from us, it is those that continue to zip in and out at strategic times, or that we use modern technology with whom to faithfully keep in correspondence. This attraction is how we walk away from an event with only those two new people added to our contact list, knowing we will be in touch, and not being overly concerned if that is not the case with the twenty, forty, or three hundred other people with whom we shared the same time and space.

No, being attracted to people, whether it be of the opposite gender or the same, is not the problem—society's hyper-sexualization of normal, healthy, intimate relationships is the problem. And deception lies at its core—deception meant to rob us of the true intimate nature of relationships in which God originally designed us to function. As I look back over my life, I recognize the attempted sabotage. This is my story:

Cycling through the mountains, our bikes heavily weighted with packs, my friend and I toured through the islands just off of the West coast. Excited to share the adventures with my students as part of a class lesson, I drew posters and eagerly recounted the tales of the trail. I did not fathom, nor could have possibly predicted the repercussions that followed because of it. The fact that my friend and I, another girl, shared a tent, became the foundation of a lie and the content of a neighboring school's locker room discussion that we were gay. What!? In my day, sharing accommodations with same-sex friends, especially when traveling with sports teams, was just logical and economical—and exceedingly necessary if you are biking through the mountains, carrying all your own gear! And yet, here it was, the basis for a rumor spread far enough to worm its way back to me.

Again the accusation came from another as I chatted in the vehicle for what he considered too long, with my *girlfriend* (in my day, this is what we called our friends who were girls, and it was never questioned or misunderstood) after our visit. "If we were sitting there together for so long … we must be making out." What!? I couldn't even guess the supposed logic that made that jump possible! (My best guess would be he was trying to shame me into giving up my friendships and create a form of isolation in my life.)

Attending a work function in place of a friend's unavailable husband again brought on the assumption and questions about the nature of our relationship. And once again, the end of a long-term relationship brought with it too, the suggestion that I had left because I could not love him —I preferred women. With this he dropped an indication that he had heard such things from others as well, thus providing his proof. This logic, at least I could follow. What other reason for me walking away would leave him looking so blameless? Though this notion was unfounded and untrue, I could understand why he would promote it.

When confronted with this issue head-on so many times, you tend to check your heart. Growing up I preferred climbing trees and playing football to playing with dolls, though I did play with those too, when my big sister made me! But this was not an anomaly at the time. I was still very much a girl. And yes, I absolutely love my same-sex friends. They are a big part of my world. I hug them when I see them, hold their hand when I pray for them, and give them the comforting touch they need when their hearts are breaking. This is called *affection*. It is normal, natural, and needed. It is in no way, sexual. Jesus was affectionate with John (John 13:25 NKJV). The sinful woman was affectionate with Jesus (Luke 7:38). We are instructed to greet our brothers with a holy kiss (1 Thessalonians 5:26). But society, under the direction of the enemy, has taken this godly affection and twisted it: *if it is attraction, it is sexual. If it is touch, it is sexual. If it is love in any form, it has to be sexual.* With society forcefully promoting this hyper-sexualized view of relationships and consciously leaving out the option of non-sexual physical affection and intimacy to meet our emotional needs, we are being coerced into the realm of lust, homosexuality, and promiscuity.

Too often I have heard the taunts of, "You're gay," as two little girls innocently hold hands or two same-sex teenagers hug in enthusiasm, planting seeds of doubt and confusion in their minds. I can see the thought process the enemy is attempting to initiate with the lie that affection and attraction has to be sexual: *I like holding my friend's hand. I like when she hugs me. I have such fun and am at peace when I hang out with her. Maybe I am gay...* This seems to become a viable option for some, as they are blinded to having their needs met through healthy, intimate relationships with both sexes the way God intended them—especially when they have trust wounds in their heart, or are lacking attention and approval from significant people in their lives.

Even the appropriate, affectionate intimacy between a loving parent and their child has been brought under the scrutiny of public debate. And in this perverse logic of over-sexualization and the sexualization of children, spun out of control, we, as a society, have been guilty of planting lies and being used by the enemy to rob us of godly intimacy—the very nature of human interaction in its original design. And this is a very dangerous road to take, leading too many young men and women onto a path of utter despair and destruction. Though this was not my story, much to the enemy's chagrin, it was the story of one young man; and I am honored to be the vehicle in which he can share his story, and save so many from the same turmoil he endured.

Emmanuel's Story

It was an ordinary day. My parents had to be somewhere, so they dropped me off at the babysitter. Everything seemed to be normal until I was taken into a room. At that point, I knew something was different. I wasn't entirely sure what was going on, but I knew I was being taken advantage of. I remember  shutting the blinds of the room. I thought to myself, *If God sees this, it'll hurt his heart too much.* I suppose God knew a lot more than my three or four-year-old mind could comprehend. In fact, God knew the pain and sorrow of the years ahead.

After the sexual abuse, I began to feel slightly different toward the same gender. I knew I felt attracted to girls, but also to boys. Since I was so young, it wasn't something to which I paid much attention. I remember one day when my parents and I were staying in a hotel. In the morning we went down to have breakfast. As we sat to eat, we watched the news, which soon changed to covering the Toronto Pride Parade. I saw two guys holding hands on t.v., and immediately, confusion entered my mind. "How is it possible that two guys can hold hands in the same way my mom and dad do?" Since I grew up in a Baptist home that taught me homosexuality was a sin, I was very scared to tell my family what I felt inside. From there, I continued to go down a path of confusion.

As the years went by in elementary school, I gained some weight, and boys began to make fun of me. They would call me fat and ugly and would exclude me from recess activities. I decided that if men were the ones who were always going to hurt me, then I would only hang out with girls, in hopes that all the name-calling would cease. However, it became worse. I began to hear, "Queer, fag, you're gay," and many other derogatory terms that are best left out. By this point, I was old enough to know what "gay" meant. I questioned myself. "Maybe I am gay? I have feelings for boys, and they're saying this is who I am without me telling them, so maybe they're right." My parents put me in karate classes as the bullying became physical, but I hated anything that had to do with fighting.

I was a very gentle and calm child, so the thought of violence repulsed me. With no way to fight for myself and no one to defend me, I felt hopeless.

In 2007 we moved out of Brampton, Ontario to Saskatchewan. I was sad to leave the very few friends I had, yet hopeful at the thought of not being bullied anymore. This was an exciting year for me. I was finally turning ten years old, a huge milestone in my mind, and I was set to visit my home country of Colombia. I had a lot of things to look forward to. I was excited to know life would only get better from here.

Unfortunately, history repeated itself, and at ten years old, I was taken advantage of sexually again. "Never tell your parents about this," said the guy who took advantage of me. At that moment, fear gripped my heart at the thought of what would happen if I told my family. For about a year after that incident, I lived in constant fear, anxiety, guilt, shame, and condemnation. I blamed myself for what had happened. I would constantly break down as I had flashbacks. I was drowning in a pool of unforgiveness while holding onto hate to keep me afloat. Little did I know it was only causing me to sink deeper. It was only when my parents found out that I felt a sense of relief.

When I was twelve years old, I decided enough was enough. The sexual abuse and bullying had followed me and nothing seemed to be getting better. I went down to the basement of my house, closed the windows, shut the door, wrapped a rope around the pipes, stood on a chair, and put the rope around my neck. "If this is all that life is, it's not worth living," I said out loud. My heart began to pound fast as I faced the reality that death was simply one step away. I slowly lifted one foot off of the chair, and was going to lift the other one, but no sooner had I lifted my foot than a gentle wind swept the room. I looked everywhere and realized the air conditioning hadn't activated and the windows were all closed. It scared me so badly that I got off that chair and figured I'd give life a second chance.

By the time I was in grade seven, I had already been a year deep into looking at homosexual pornography. The bullying had thankfully subsided, but new struggles were emerging. In grade eight, my friends introduced me to chat rooms. At first, it seemed innocent and fun to talk to random strangers around the world and meet new people. I started to realize these rooms might take me down a bad path. I desperately needed change.

During the summer of my grade nine year, I had an opportunity to take part in a youth summer mission's program called "Street Invaders." I started to encounter God in a powerful way. I witnessed God supernaturally heal my physical body, and I witnessed Him heal other people as I prayed for them. During this time I questioned God if He was so good, why He wouldn't have stopped all the terrible things I've had to walk through. God took me back to the garden, where it all began. He showed me the free will He gave us, and how man chose that free will to sin and has continued to do so ever since. I walked away from Street Invaders with pain in my heart, but with a new sense of purpose. Perhaps I was on earth to display the wonders of Jesus and lead people to Him. It's these experiences that served as an anchor to the realities of God. Due to what I saw and experienced at Street Invaders, it kept me from walking away from God and denying His existence.

After Street Invaders, I started grade ten feeling hopeful, yet still struggling with pornography. By this point, my outward appearance was developing and I was gaining attention from homosexual men in these chat rooms. I started to enjoy the attention I was getting, so it had me coming back for more. Eventually, this turned into me performing sexual acts online for these guys. I began to lose all sense of worth in my life.

Grade eleven would be the greatest, yet the worst year of my life. I had just come back from a mission trip with Street Invaders to the Philippines where I had seen God move in great ways. When I returned, I went back to all my old, sinful habits. One day when I was in the chat rooms, I met a guy who lived not too far from where I lived. We continued to talk a lot as the months followed and we became very close. A few months into the friendship, he told me he had feelings for me. Since I knew homosexuality was a sin, I told him I could be his friend, but nothing else. Eventually, I realized I was having feelings for this guy too. Depression polluted my life as fear entangled me. I began to harm myself physically and hated myself for the feelings I was having. I was trapped in a cage of uncertainty, longing to be delivered, but too afraid to ask for freedom.

I ended up reaching out to a close friend I had at the time. She took me to a church in my city that was pastored by a man who was married to another man. This concept was totally foreign to me. A practicing homosexual pastor? I didn't even know that was possible. I sat down with this pastor and he shared with me his theological view in regard to homosexuality. I remember thinking he was so deeply deceived. I couldn't believe anyone would twist Scripture so much to come to the conclusion that homosexuality wasn't a sin.

I walked away from that meeting and a thought came to me. "What if he's right and I'm wrong? What if the church as a whole is wrong for their conservative view on marriage?" A seed of deception was planted in my heart. I decided he was right, and I would finally live the way I wanted to live. I was proud to finally accept myself for who I was and start a relationship with this guy for whom I had deep feelings.

I became involved with this young man emotionally and sexually. I thought I had finally found love. I felt I had discovered my purpose in life: to show the church that you can be actively gay and serve God. I wanted to show them how terribly deceived they were for believing homosexuality is a sin. I had deeply hardened my heart and built a wall in front of me that prevented me from seeing the truth. Behind this wall, lust masqueraded itself as love, and lies choked the life out of the truth. Every desire and dream that I had to be married to a woman and raise a family was completely crushed under the weight of despair. I was really good at making it seem like I was happy, but deep down I was hurting.

I decided it was time to tell my church, Christian school, and my family, the life I was living. I was prepared to get kicked out of every Christian community I was a part of. However, to my surprise, my church and school loved me and accepted me, yet they never backed down on what they believed to be true. This caused a great desire in me to know the truth. I had secular friends who were very excited for the decisions I had made to live an active homosexual lifestyle, and I had my family in Christ who deeply loved me, yet shared the truth of God's Word with me, that strongly opposed my secular friends' views. I was dealing with a lot of confusion, depression, fear, and suicidal thoughts. In the midst of all this, I once again attempted suicide to no avail. I desperately needed a Savior.

Everyone that ever spoke the truth of God's Word into my life, grabbed a sledgehammer and took a swing at that wall I had built up. Eventually, the wall came completely down. I remember sitting with a good friend of mine during lunch break. I asked her what she thought about the way I was living. She told me she believed homosexuality was a sin, and marriage was between one man and one woman. She told me everything else I've heard other Christians speak to me. I thanked her for sharing this with me, but I made sure she knew I strongly disagreed. Once the bell rang, I grabbed my gym clothes and headed to the gym.

As soon as I entered the gym, tears began to flow down my face. I was unsure why, so I went into the bathroom to try to compose myself. I spent the next hour on the ground in the bathroom crying, kicking, and punching the walls. I wasn't sure why I was in this deep emotional state, but I remember yelling, "God, take care of him!!!" referring to the guy I was in a relationship with. Later that evening I went into the prayer room at my church and the Lord spoke to me. I saw a vision of Him stretching out His hand, and He said, "Emmanuel, do you trust Me enough to take My hand through this journey, even though you have no idea how it's going to end?" I told God I was choosing to trust Him. I went to go see my youth pastor where I spent an hour crying in her office. I was then introduced to the inner healing ministry offered by my church.

I began my inner healing journey with two questions, "Is homosexuality a sin?" and "What do You want me to do, God?" Over the next few months, God began to pick  up the broken pieces of my heart and put it together. He began to heal me of being bullied, sexually abused, depressed, and all the other cuts I had in my life. On April 16, 2014, I was sitting in my room and I asked God to speak to me. I saw a vision of a door. I saw a hand reach out and lock the door. The next day during my inner healing session, all I could see was this door. We began to ask the Lord to show more and the Lord expanded on this vision. Everything was pitch dark around me, except this door that had been locked; it had a light on top. As I started to walk toward the door, fluorescent lights appeared on the side of the hallway that had written on it, "Queer, fag, worthless," and every other word that had been spoken over me. When I approached the door, the vision paused, and I saw someone very dark in presence taking care of me as a baby. He was doing something to me, but I couldn't quite tell what. This man was very excited to see me approach the door and walk through it. I stood in front of the door and asked God what was behind it. The Lord showed the guy I was in a relationship with and the destruction that would come by living a homosexual lifestyle. Since there was nowhere else to go, I stretched out my hand to unlock the door to walk through it.

Just before I nearly touched the door, a hallway lit up, bright as day, to my right. I heard the audible voice of God say, "Run!" The second every part of me stepped out of the dark hallway and into the light, the light on top of the door, along with the fluorescent lights, shut off with a great sound like lights turning off in a football stadium. As I ran, this man that took care of me as a baby was getting angry, so he threw hurdles in front of me so I would trip. In the vision, I ran fast and jumped over these hurdles. The further I ran away from the door, the less I felt attracted to the same gender. At one point I tripped over a hurdle. As soon as I looked back, I saw a little night lamp by the door. The Lord said, "Emmanuel, I've only locked that door. You can turn to it whenever you want and unlock it, but now you know what I have for you." As I looked back I began to feel attraction to the same gender surge through me once again. At the very end of the vision, this man who was taking care of me was trying to blow the vision out of my mind. Then, a stamp came down over the vision in big, bold, black letters dripping with blood that said, "Redemption."

After this vision, I chose to end the relationship I was in. I continued coming to inner healing to break soul ties and continued to allow God to heal my heart. God then began to restore the dreams I had of marrying a woman and raising a family. He began to restore my passion for ministry and for doing great things for Him. I still struggled with temptation, and at times would trip over the hurdles and take some steps back. However, I kept coming back to Jesus for forgiveness and cutting ties with any habits I was falling back into.

Though I tried to stay away from falling into temptation in person with another guy, the internet seemed to be a constant stumble for me. I decided to put up lots of boundaries, and get accountability. In my time of looking back at the door, I continued to feel attracted to the same gender. However, it's been a while now since I have turned back to any of those old habits, and I can't express the level of joy and freedom I feel in my heart. The more I run from this door in my life, the less the feelings for the same gender feel true.

After leaving the homosexual lifestyle, my mind was polluted with memories of the things I've watched, the music I have listened to, and the things I've done. It seemed like I was always getting bombarded with thoughts from the past. Over a period of six months, I went through a purging of thoughts. I prayed a simple prayer out loud that has dramatically changed my thought-life. The prayer went something like this, "Father forgive me for exposing myself to … (name the sinful thought, movie scene, song, etc.) I renounce that in my life. Seal that door in my life with Your blood, in Jesus' name." Each time thoughts came up after that, I would simply say out loud, "I rebuke that thought in Jesus' name." These two simple prayers helped me to clear away a lot of the junk stored in my heart. It was also very important in my life to become very careful with the music I listened to, the movies I watched, etc.

Over the years, I've been able to step more into the calling God has placed on my life. I give glory to God for the hundreds of people I've had the opportunity to lead to Jesus and the hundreds that have encountered physical healing in their bodies. I no longer walk around aimlessly seeking love, acceptance, and value. I'm a new person. That doesn't mean life is perfect. This just simply means that as struggles and temptations arise, I turn to Jesus to be my strength and hope.

My prayer is that you find great encouragement, strength, and hope for whatever you may be walking through in your own healing journey. Revelation 19:10 says, "Then I fell down at his feet to worship him, but he said to me, 'You must not do that! I am a fellow servant with you and your brothers who hold to the testimony of Jesus. Worship God.' For the testimony of Jesus is the spirit of prophecy." Simply put, what it's saying is, whatever Jesus has done in the past, He will do it again. Jesus has radically changed my life. He breathed life into dead dreams and passions. He's been changing ungodly desires and replacing them with the desires He created. No matter what you're walking through, if He did it for me, He can do it for you. Don't give up, He sure hasn't.

Be healed, in Jesus' name!

Thank you, Emmanuel, for sharing your story. It touched my heart. I pray God's continued blessings on you.

In my reflections on this area, I began to question why the enemy has chosen to expend so many of his resources to pervert human sexuality. There are many obvious ramifications to sexual sin, including the destruction of marriage and the family, preventing us from having the clean hands and pure heart as so desired by the Lord, and its defiling nature to the body (which is intended to be glorified as the temple of the Holy Spirit).

But hidden amongst these ones was an unexpected revelation. If the devil can distort and corrupt our understanding of the true nature of intimate relationships, he will effectively rob us of the exact relationship Jesus desires to have with each one of us. If we are deceived into believing intimacy is always sexual and *can only be* sexual, how then, can we have an intimate relationship with Jesus, God the Father, or Holy Spirit? This bondage of corruption therefore has not only the potential to steal human relationships, but the divine. There is much at stake. It is time to take back our territory in the area of human sexuality.

Pushing Up

A. Clean Hands and a Pure Heart

The Father wants to restore purity to your whole being—body, soul, and spirit. Repentance wipes the slate clean, and allows you to stand in front of the Father in full righteousness, because of the blood of Jesus and the finished work of the cross. It also closes the open spiritual door that allows for enemy attacks against you and your family. As hard as this next step is, it is necessary. Sexual sin has a devastating impact on us and our family—body, soul, and spirit. Only by facing our sin, repenting for it, and turning from its enticement, can we truly be set free from the bondage of its corruption.

Prayer:

Dear Lord, thank You for being concerned about every area of my being, including my sexuality. You know, oh so well, how much damage can be done to a person's soul in this vulnerable area. You want me to have clean hands and a pure heart. I want to have clean hands and a pure heart, so I am fit for Your service—a vessel of gold and silver, refined by Your fire. Help me to be transparent and honest with myself and with You. Holy Spirit, please bring revelation as to any of my actions, thoughts, and behaviors that have not been pleasing to You. Restore any forgotten memories You wish me to have, and repress anything that would be damaging to me at this point of my healing.

I cancel every word curse spoken over me by anyone, known or unknown, with unholy sexual intentions toward me. I come out of alignment with every word curse with sexual content I have spoken over myself. I repent for any impure words I have spoken over myself or another. I cancel every assignment of the enemy that has fought to steal my purity. I ask You, Jesus, to wash me with Your blood, ridding me of any unholy sexual thing deposited on me by my thoughts and actions or those of another toward me. (Wash your body clean in a prophetic gesture. Use water symbolically if you feel the need to do so.)

On a separate piece of paper, write out your sexual sins. Include thoughts, attitudes, ideals, and beliefs, as revealed to you by Holy Spirit. **Confess these sins to God, repenting and renouncing—turning from them—one by one.** If you struggle in this area, I also suggest confessing them to a trusted confidant. As seemingly difficult as this is, it brings accountability into your life. **Burn, shred, or otherwise destroy the paper, releasing these past sins unto the Lord, and thank Him that HE HAS FORGIVEN YOU for every one of them.**

(Continue with the prayer:)

I repent for everything I have exposed myself to, exposed others to, or that others have exposed me to that were not in line with the purity You ask of me, including reading material, images, movies, music, and objects. I break all soul ties with them. Please cancel their effects, and remove any poison they have placed in my body and mind. Heal me from any trauma I have incurred as I was exposed to them. Rewire my brain and wash it clean with Your blood! I renounce further interaction with them. Seal any doors of sexuality that are not pleasing to You with the blood of the Lamb! I break any chains of sexual bondage formed by sexual sin.

Help me hunger after purity and make godly choices in entertainment, behavior, relationships, and information. Restore to me my innocence and purity. I want to experience relationships in their fulness as You intended them to be. I ask You to give me a true understanding of love and godly sex. Open my eyes to see the damage sexual immorality brings to my life and the lives of those around me. Help me to be an example of sexual purity and a pillar of strength to encourage others to live a life of purity, giving purity its due honor. Give me the courage to tell my story to others as You lead me, to bring healing into their lives. Guard my mind from impure thoughts. Help me to rebuke them the moment they surface. Guard my soul as I sleep. Keep my dreams pure and holy; receiving only instruction from You in my slumber.

I break off every spirit of shame, guilt, condemnation, confusion, fear, death, destruction, seduction, lust, blame, anxiety, despair, and depression that have attached themselves to me. I repent for partnering with them and believing their lies. GO NOW, IN THE NAME OF JESUS! I CAST YOU ALL OUT! I PUT THE CROSS OF CHRIST BETWEEN ME AND EVERY ONE OF THESE SPIRITS AND I CANCEL THEIR ASSIGNMENTS! I declare myself free from them by the power of the shed blood of the Lamb, Jesus Christ. I am redeemed, cleansed, and restored by the washing with Your blood. Lord, I ask You to fill every empty spot in me with Your purity, peace, joy, understanding, life, love, and hope. Place a guard of purity around me, that the enemy cannot sway me with his accusations, deceit, temptations, and enticements.

Lord, right now I stand in the gap for my loved ones (name them) and repent for any sexual sin on their behalf until they can do so on their own. Bring them to that place where they too, can come before You in humbleness and gratitude, and receive Your forgiveness. I pray this in the holy name of Jesus Christ of Nazareth. Amen

Is God asking you to lay anything or anyone down on the altar?

_____
_____
_____

B. Triage

There may be some things in our lives that have happened to us that were too ugly for us to want to remember them—so we don't. We thus bury them deeply into the dark recesses of our mind, locking them forever away, so they don't hurt us any more. The only problem is that though we do not even remember them, or we consciously choose to keep them locked away, they are still hurting us. They still produce toxic thoughts, behaviors, and reactions, whether we acknowledge the existence of the original wound or not. We believe we have left it behind for the better—but it has not left us behind. It eventually oozes out in unexpected ways and infects the rest of our lives, and the lives of those around us.

As hateful as walking through painful memories may seem, sometimes it is necessary. Other times, the Lord will bring healing with a word of knowledge, without a memory attached. You may not need to recall any specific details, or even the event itself. In His wisdom and under

His guidance, you can trust Him to direct your course to bring about the healing necessary in your life.

Ask Holy Spirit if there have been any incidents in your life where you have been sexually abused or taken advantage of that need to be addressed at this point in your healing journey. Remember, your definition of *abuse* and God's may differ—God does not minimize, justify or rationalize—we do. You may remember the incident immediately, or it may be buried. The memory may seem too trivial to you to have caused any damage, or it may seem so great that it cannot be taken out of its secret place. But trust Him. He is bringing it to mind for a reason and He will give you the courage and strength you need to walk through it. You may have already prayed about it and feel there has been healing, but if it is brought to your mind, there may be a part of it still needing to be brought to full resolution; or perhaps the Lord wants to take your healing to a deeper level.

Sometimes, the Lord will only reveal such things as a time period, a place, or even a person, but no memory. Pray this revelation through as you would a specific memory, as your body still remembers and may be carrying the trauma, even though your mind does not necessarily recall the event. You can still receive healing, whether you eventually remember the specific event or not. In His wisdom, the Lord will deem some events best not remembered.

If no specific incidents are brought to remembrance, yet you can see things in your life that lead you to belief you have a wounding in this area, pray with a trusted friend. You may require additional prayer support and are not to open this area without God's hands in the physical around you through the process.

Prayer:
Dear Holy Spirit, You know my life better than I do. You know all, even things I have chosen to forget, or have never even known, right back to my conception. I ask You now to speak to my heart in the tender area of sexual abuse. Please reveal to me if there have been any incidents, known to me or not, where I have been abused or taken advantage of in any manner. Please reveal all things that need to be revealed at this stage of my healing journey, and keep hidden any

things that should remain hidden, until the time comes that You say they should be brought to the light. I give You permission to disclose everything necessary, according to Your perfect timing. I ask for the grace, strength, and determination to walk through all You bring to my attention, no matter how painful. I know You have healing and freedom for me and my family as I lay it all before You.

Record His revelations on the following pages.

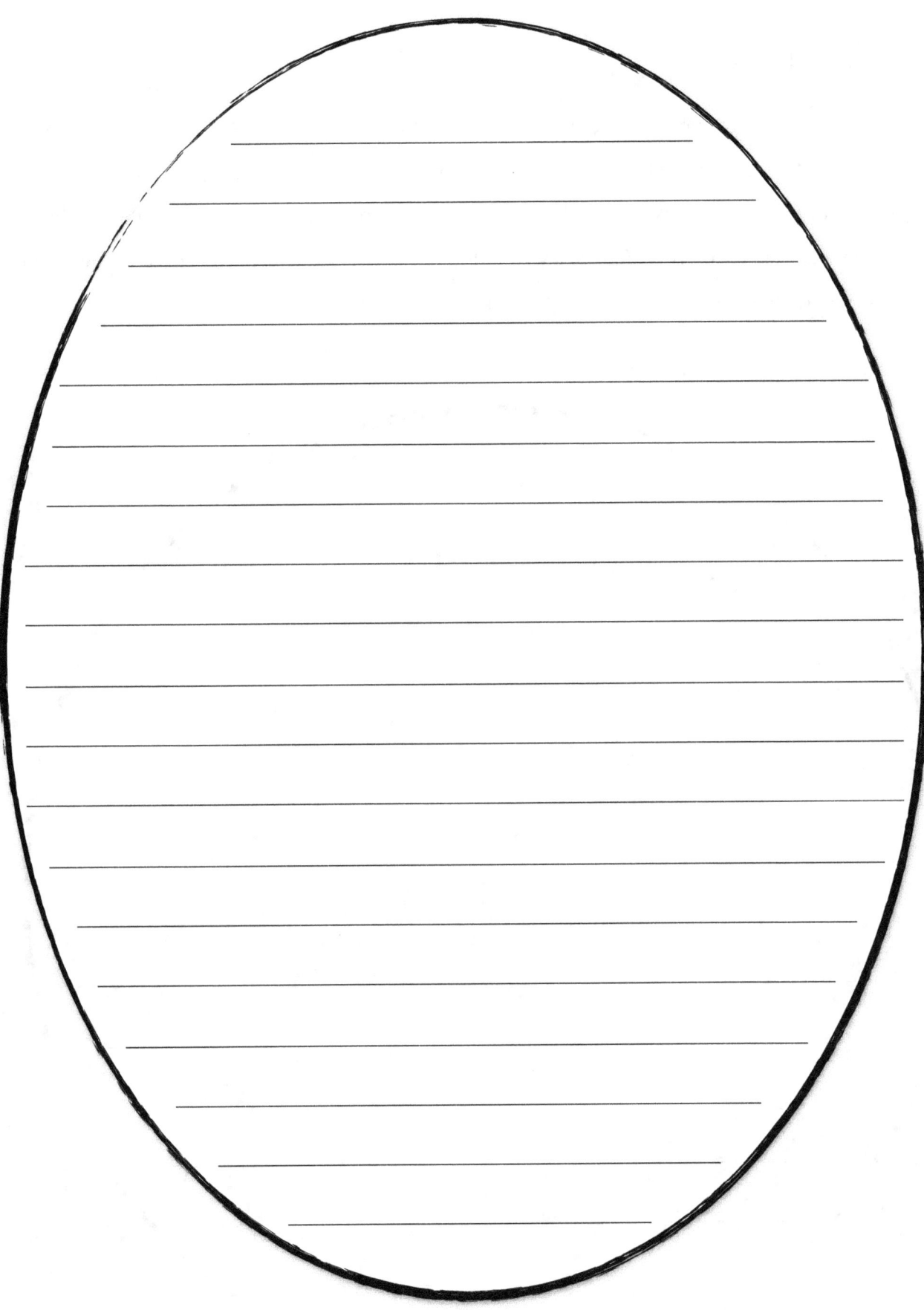

C. Flipping Tables

Feelings are not to direct your course, but they do need to be expressed. As you look back over these things that have happened to you, how does it make you feel? It is okay to be sad and even angry. Take time to grieve, express righteous anger, question God, and express other feelings associated with these memories of abuse. Write, draw, scream, cry, scribble ... do what you need to do to be heard, to give yourself a voice, and to take back your "NO!

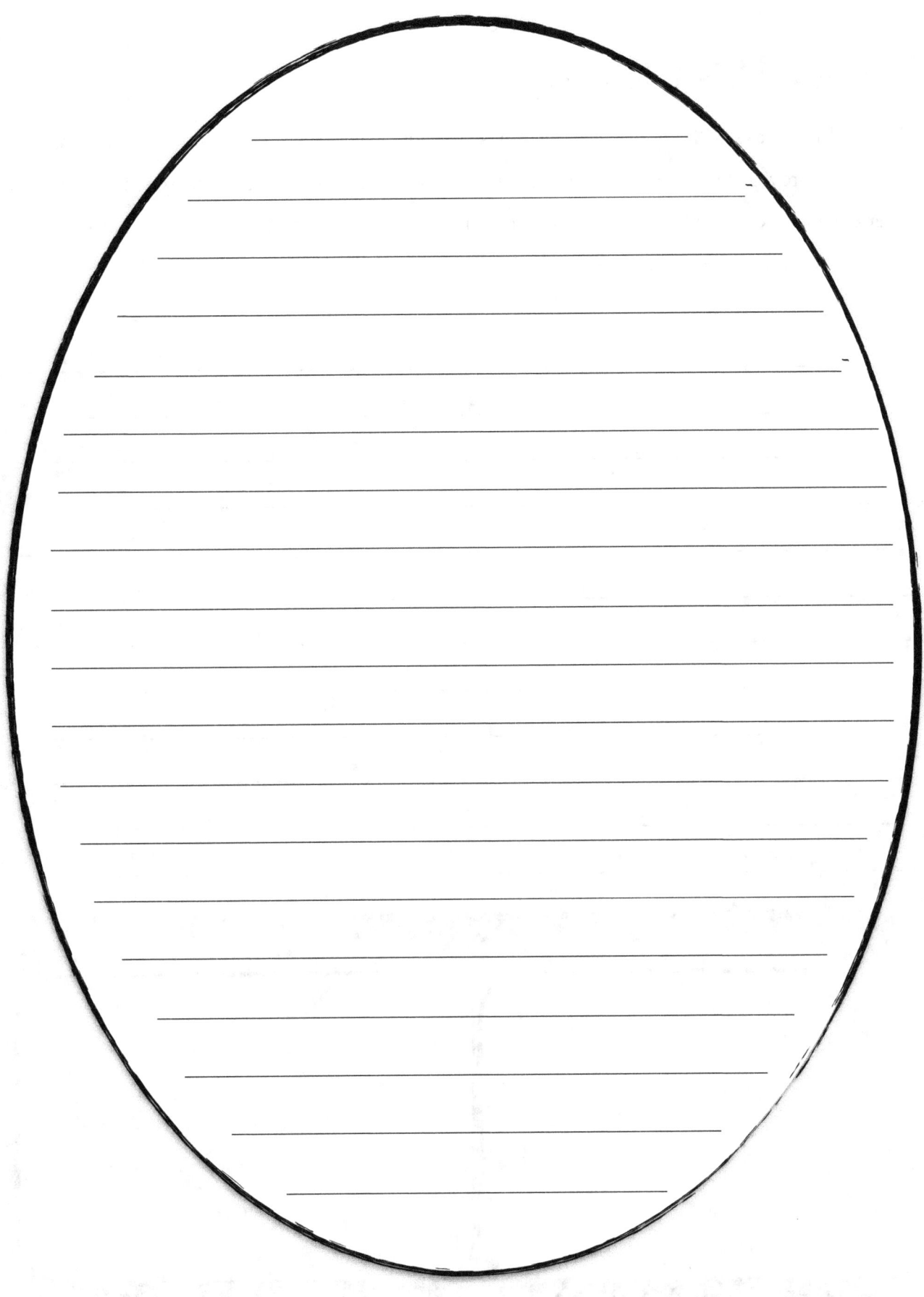

D. Where WERE You, Jesus?

The Lord is always with us, even in our times of trauma—we just cannot always see Him. Ask the Lord to reveal to you where He was during your trials of enduring the sexual abuse you experienced. Ask Him what He was doing, and how He helped you. Record His revelation to You in words, Scripture and/or pictures.

E. Healing Dialogue

On the following pages, write a prayer to the Lord asking for healing. Follow the suggested outline, and add in any specifics, as per suggestions by Holy Spirit. As you craft the prayer, give time for Holy Spirit to reveal the needed areas before you continue to dialogue with the Lord through your prayer. Include these revelations as a part of your prayer.

★ Thank the Lord for being with you in your trauma.

★ Ask Jesus to heal every wound inflicted upon you through sexual abuse.

★ Ask the Lord to heal the memories and your scars.

★ Ask Holy Spirit to reveal to you any specific places in which trauma from these events is being held in your body. (Record His revelations.)

★ Ask the Lord to remove all trauma stored anywhere in your body, and specifically in every place the Lord revealed, and bring healing and life, returning to you all you had lost.

★ Ask the Lord to resurrect any parts of you that had died with the abuse.

★ Ask Holy Spirit for revelation of any thought patterns or behaviors in which you are trapped because of abuse. (Record His revelations.)

★ Ask the Lord to cleanse your mind and reset your thought patterns, specifically standing against any negative patterns you have developed as a result of abuse, as revealed by Holy Spirit. If you have used sex as a means of power, control, or acceptance, repent from this and surrender it unto the Lord.

★ Ask the Lord to seal the work done in your heart.

I Give Voice to my Heart ...

F. Removing the Darkness

To let in the light of healing requires the removal of darkness. Holding onto unforgiveness against those who have hurt us, taken advantage of us, and abused us keeps the darkness in our own hearts and prevents healing. Forgiving does not mean trusting them; nor does it excuse or condone their actions. Forgiveness means handing them over to the Father for Him to deal with them as He chooses. It means not harboring bitterness or vengeance in our souls against them, which only hardens our own hearts. It means letting go of our hatred toward them. And forgiving these ones releases them to receive their own healing, understanding that they hurt us out of their own deep woundedness. As we forgive them, we too, are released into our own healing.

Is there anyone you need to forgive? _____

Say a prayer of forgiveness over them, releasing yourself and them into healing. At times the Lord will ask you to forgive them in person. Be open to this if He so asks of you. It is a hard step to take, but the freedom and the strength you will gain in your obedience will be worth it. If your head is telling you to forgive someone, but your heart won't budge, say the words in simple obedience, even if you don't *feel like* it is true forgiveness.

In time, with your obedience, the Lord will connect the words confessed out of your mouth with your heart. And every time anger or hatred rise up in you against the person, continue to walk through forgiving them. Be determined. It is a process, but after a while, it becomes easier and easier, and the time span between saying the words and believing them in your heart becomes shorter. And with each step you take in forgiveness, the Lord strengthens you and gives you more authority in the heavenly realm.

Is there anyone you have hurt in your woundedness from whom you need to ask for forgiveness? Ask Holy Spirit if there are any actions you need to take to make restitution.

_____
_____

G. Tearing Down Lies

You have been hurt too long by the lies the enemy planted in your mind at the times of abuse, or following thereafter, in attempts to reinforce his warped perspective. It is time to recognize the truth of who God says you are in the area of sexuality, and to understand your true worth as the Bride of Christ. You may believe you are dirty, shameful, unworthy, unloveable, or damaged because of the things that have happened to you, or because of past choices you have made or that have been forced upon you. You may believe your value is tied to sexual acts, gender, or sexuality. Some of these lies may have been attacking the foundational identity of your gender and sexuality. You may feel it is not safe for you to be a female or a male. You may feel you cannot trust a specific gender. You may have cited such inner vows as, "I will never let a man/woman touch me. I will never trust a man/woman."

Ask Holy Spirit to reveal any lies planted in your heart at the time of the abuse, or since, because of abuse. What does your heart tell you about your sexuality?

_____
_____
_____
_____

Ask Holy Spirit to tear down the lies by exposing the truth about who you are in the area of sexuality.

_____
_____
_____
_____

Come out of alignment with the lies and realign with God's truth, as brought to light on the previous page.

Prayer:

I come out of alignment with the lie _____

The truth is _____

I come out of alignment with the lie _____

The truth is _____

I come out of alignment with the lie _____

The truth is _____

Did you make any inner vows in the area of sexuality or gender to keep yourself safe?
What did your heart tell you? *I will never … I will always … I need to …*

_____
_____
_____
_____
_____

Prayer:

I cancel the vow that …

I will instead trust that …

Continue the prayer with each vow.

H. Restoration into the Truth

Spend some quiet time with the Lord, reflecting on all you have learned, and the healing you have received. Ask God to speak to your heart, showing you His perspective of who you are in the fulness of who He created you to be. Listen, really listen to what He says.

THIS IS HOW THE LORD SEES ME, KNOWS ME TO BE, ACCEPTS ME, AND LOVES ME!

His Truth

The Lord is calling us to be vessels of honor. Let His Word speak the truth of this into your heart and help you to walk in His high calling. Highlight any words and phrases with which you need to engage to become a vessel of honor.

Purge me with hyssop, and I shall be clean; wash me, and I shall be whiter than snow. Create in me a clean heart, O God, and renew a right spirit within me.

Psalm 51:7, 10

… though your sins are like scarlet, they shall be as white as snow; though they are red like crimson, they shall become like wool.

Isaiah 1:18

Who shall ascend the hill of the LORD? And who shall stand in his holy place? He who has clean hands and a pure heart, who does not lift up his soul to what is false and does not swear deceitfully. He will receive blessing from the LORD and righteousness from the God of his salvation.

Psalm 24:3-5

And everyone who thus hopes in him purifies himself as he is pure. Everyone who makes a practice of sinning also practices lawlessness; sin is lawlessness. You know that he appeared in order to take aways sins, and in him there is no sin. No one who abides in him keeps on sinning; no one who keeps on sinning has either seen him or known him.

1 John 3:3-6

Therefore, beloved, since you are waiting for these, be diligent to be found by him without spot or blemish, and at peace.

2 Peter 3:14

Put to death therefore what is earthly in you: sexual immorality, impurity, passion, evil desire, and covetousness, which is idolatry. On account of these the wrath of God is coming. In these you too once walked, when you were living in them. But now you must put them all away: anger, wrath, malice, slander, and obscene talk from your mouth.

Colossians 3:5-8

For this is the will of God, our sanctification: that you abstain from sexual immorality; that each one of you know how to control his own body in holiness and honor, not in the passion of lust like the Gentiles who do not know God …

1 Thessalonians 4:3-5

To the pure, all things are pure, but to the defiled and unbelieving, nothing is pure; but both their minds and their consciences are defiled. They profess to know God, but they deny him by their works. They are detestable, disobedient, unfit for any good work.

Titus 1:15-16

But if we walk in the light, as he is in the light, we have fellowship with one another, and the blood of Jesus his Son cleanses us from all sin.

1 John 1:7

Blessed are the pure in heart, for they shall see God.

Matthew 5:8

Declaring His Truth

Write a declaration calling you into becoming a vessel of silver and gold; a vessel of honor, sanctified and useful for the Master, prepared for every good work.

Use the Scripture phrases you highlighted to guide the crafting of the declaration.

Unit Seven

The Enemy's Bitter Fruit

> Your words were found, and I ate them, and your words became to me a joy and the delight of my heart, for I am called by your name, O LORD, God of hosts.
>
> Jeremiah 15:16

IMAGINE YOURSELF CROSSING A BRIDGE SUSPENDED HIGH ABOVE A ROCKY MOUNTAIN GORGE, where one false step could determine your fate. The ropes, worn and frayed, do nothing to bolster your confidence in its safety. The rotting wooden slats, spaced far apart, make the jagged rocks down below easily visible, emphasizing the risk of each step. Sadly, this is the way many of us have chosen to live our lives—as our thoughts, decisions, and situations daily torment us with the insecurity of the path on which we walk.

Yet this is not what the Lord offers to us. This is not His chosen way. I, walking this route myself, admittedly used to become so frustrated when one of my many counselors would sum up my supposedly complicated situation with "So … you are not trusting Jesus then …" Simple truth. One morning, the Lord showed me how I was walking through life as if I was hanging in mid-air on this terrifying bridge. Suddenly, in my mind, I saw God take the bridge and lay it on a huge cement pad. Same rickety bridge. Same path. Firm foundation. It made all the difference.

The very first prophetic word I had given to me described the foundation of lies (the rickety bridge) on which I had built my life; only at the time, I didn't know they were lies.

Prophetic word - December 2009
Jocelyn, I had such a strong impression over you … makes me want to start crying … just a broken-heartedness. I feel your heart has been broken many times over. I see much crying, weeping before the Lord … many times. I can almost hear you saying to the Lord, "How many times am I going to be in this place of disappointment …" … a place where you started to get your hopes and dreams built up again and then it is like they keep shattering and keep falling apart.

I feel like in the past there's been confusion in your mind in terms of what's happening, the circumstances you've been in, and I see God wanting to bring strength and more solidness and stability into your life. It is like a rebuilding of a foundation in your life. I felt like you thought you had a foundation, but when it came to the trials and the winds of adversity coming against you it crumbled. It didn't hold you on solid ground. I think that has brought confusion in your life and so there is a rebuilding process that has been going on in your relationship with the Lord.

I see God placing cement blocks before you that would speak of being able to walk on something solid. I see Him placing them ahead of you for you to take one step at a time. As you are doing that He's wanting to increase your stability. I see a firmer foundation being rebuilt in your life, and yet all this time you are wrestling with a lack of trust and an insecurity because it is like you thought you had something you didn't have … you thought you had a foundation and it didn't turn out to be that way, so I see things falling to pieces and creating a big mistrust inside of you.

I feel God is going to restore the hope inside of you to say it is okay for you to dream again, it is okay for you to hang on to those foundation stones He is putting in front of you. You can trust in them and they are not going to fall into the sinking sand like the last time around. And it almost seems to me like you had a sense of how to build your life, but that is the thing that fell apart. God is wanting to give you new, established ways of walking and ways of standing, and I feel like this time as you are rooted in the Lord, you are not going to be blown over.

God is changing you— where you are like a tree that a wind can really come against it, and can really bend it over, but it does not snap off at the base. I feel like God is rooting you in such a way that adversity is not going to affect you the way it used to. I see you becoming a different person than you used to be. And as you are able to trust in God and in the foundation He is going to build in your life, I really see it is like the weeping woman being cast off of you ...
—Diane Harrison

GROWING UP I HAD ALWAYS ASSUMED I'D HAVE WHAT I CONSIDERED A *REGULAR LIFE* AS I crossed into adulthood; much like what I'd experienced in my own childhood and witnessed in the lives of those around me. I pictured getting married and having a few kids. Summers would be spent camping and boating. Perhaps we'd even have a cottage. Winter vacations to somewhere hot were a part of the dream. Both having successful, fulfilling careers, we'd send the kids off to the college of their choice, and my husband and I would retire, spending our time holding hands as we swung on the porch swing watching the sunset.

My life did not turn out that way—at all. I did have the marriage and the kids. I still have the kids. We divorced just shy of ten years and began our lives again in the reality of all that is entailed in a broken marriage: broken lives, broken hearts, broken dreams.

I had given my life to the Lord at eighteen years of age, though had always been aware of His reality. There were times I felt I had walked closely by His side, yet chose a wider berth during those other times. I believed I knew what it meant to live the Christian life. I had attended church fairly regularly. I went on mission trips, attended Bible school, and worked with various kids' clubs and youth groups over the years. I worshipped, prayed, and I read my Bible, though not always consistently.

I thought I had a firm foundation on which to build my life. Yet admittedly, I still let my own desires influence my choices and decisions, and eventually, I became frustrated, to confess it bluntly, that God was not giving me *what I wanted*. Turning from Him in rebellion, I put my trust in *self*, and followed the ways of the world. No longer heeding His guidance, ignoring His instruction, I chose my own path. I had more fear of not getting my earthly desires met than I had fear in the Lord. Then life as I knew it, as I had hoped and dreamed it would be ... crumbled to ruins past repair. I was dismantled, brick by brick until almost nothing was left—shattered beyond recognition. Yet this very dismantling of my being became—in some ways, after much (much!) struggle and heart-ache—life-giving.

If I wanted to keep breathing, and I did because of my kids, I needed to begin a new journey; at first in search of my own healing, and then just in search of the Lord, who then brought about my healing. As I learned to trust Him, becoming vulnerable even when I felt raw, He put me back together piece by piece, rebuilding the entire structure of me, creating me to be how He intended me to be in His original design. And this time, He also set me on a firm foundation. This foundation of bedrock only comes from deeply trusting God in everything, with everything, and for everything. And this level of trust can only be developed by living in close relationship with the Lord, in His wisdom and under His instruction and guidance.

Years ago I *thought* I had known what it was like to be in relationship with the Lord. I *thought* I knew how to walk with Him and how to hear His voice. Now I *know* ... all those years ... I had absolutely *no idea*! The depth of relationship with Him in which I now walk has taught me that I had such a lack of understanding of the intimacy available to all those who seek, truly seek Him. I had no idea how much He speaks to us—how clearly we can hear His voice—if only we take the time to listen! I am just now beginning to understand the peace, joy, hope, and excitement in which we can walk as we learn to fear Him (keeping Him in that elevated place of majesty and reverence), trust Him, obey Him, and follow Him with our whole heart.

My story is not unique nor surprising, especially to God. In Isaiah 30:8-14, God has clearly laid out how in our rebellion, we make plans contrary to those of God. We neglect to consult Him but instead choose to put our trust in ourselves, other people, and things. We have refused to pay attention to the Lord's instruction, preferring not to be told what is right. We want to be told what we *desire* is right—the wide path of the world rather than the narrow path of following the Lord. We choose to despise the Holy One and instead trust in oppression and lies; even though God has blatantly foretold of the devastating results of this: calamity will come upon us and we will be smashed and shattered like a piece of pottery.

Proverbs chapters 1-4 also detail the repercussions of refusing to heed the wisdom and instruction of the Lord. (I see this description as parallel to a protective parent warning a child to adhere to their commands and thus avoid reaping the natural consequences of such things as running into traffic or sticking a metal object into a light socket.) Terror, distress, anguish, shame, death, and destruction are the explicit outcomes of following an ungodly path. Once we are aware of this, we definitely cannot claim ignorance as to the results of rebellious decisions. We see this devastation reflected all around us in society as a whole.

There is more chronic anxiety in the lives of adults, teens, and even children than ever before, in and out of the church body. (How could one *not* be *flooded* with anxiety as we traverse life in such an unstable, precarious position as this insecure, dilapidated, mid-air, foundationless suspension bridge affords us!) Too many of us walk in depression, hatred, cruelty, jealousy, envy, and sexual immorality. Betrayal, deceitfulness, infidelity, callousness, and crudeness are commonalities of behavior. Chaos, self-gratification, mental disorders, obesity, confusion, abuse, violence, and narcissism are not only a way of life for many outside of our faith, but have stealthily and steadily crept within Christian boundaries and are often left unaddressed.

But these behaviors and conditions are not the plan for the life of a believer. They are not a part of our original biology, personal identity, nor our identity in Christ. Yet we have fallen victim to the lies of the enemy that dictate they are a part of who we are and what we do, and we therefore have to live within their constraints, tolerating them in ourselves and others, and even celebrating them. Though we may be struggling in some of these areas at present, we do not have to accept that this is where we must remain. This is a mass web of deception. These behaviors and conditions are the bitter fruit of us, or those around us, living in our own way, seeking to fulfill only our own fleshly desires. We are receiving the fill of our own devices (Proverbs 1:31 ESV, NLT). In other words, we are drowning in the fruit of the enemy, produced by following his ways, (or others around us that follow his ways and inflict wounds and trauma upon us), rather than following the instruction manual of the One who has created us.

No, living with anxiety, depression, fear, confusion, and the like is not the plan for a follower of Jesus. The Lord's way is to live life in the Spirit, on a firm foundation. In doing so, we exchange hatred, depression, and anxiety for love, joy, and peace. The frustration, cruelty, and wickedness engulfing us become patience, kindness, and goodness. Betrayal and infidelity transform into faithfulness; harsh temperaments soften into gentleness, and the chaotic, self-indulgent, confused lifestyles come under self-control. This is the path God offers. Will you choose it?

Prophetic Journal Entry - July 2015

My heart strings sing at your obedience. Facing your fear, laying it all down at My feet is how we work together, My child. I will carry you when You are at My feet. That is when I can carry you—humbled, at My feet, fully trusting Me for every breath you take! That is when I can fully release My gifts to you. That is when I can fully work in you. That is how I work best, when you are fully submitted to me—fear, anxiety, pain—all of it. You trust Me with everything, then I can be your everything.

—Jesus

Pushing Up

A. Walking in Repentance

The bitter fruit produced by the enemy is easily unveiled by directly contrasting it with the fruit of the Spirit in Galatians 5:22-23, as the enemy comes in the opposite spirit. Though this list is not exhaustive, it should provide a solid point of reference. Holy Spirit, as always, will fill in any blanks!

love	joy	peace	patience	kindness
➤ hatred	➤ depression	➤ anxiety	➤ agitation	➤ cruelty
➤ animosity	➤ sadness	➤ disharmony	➤ frustration	➤ harshness
➤ antagonism	➤ sorrow	➤ discord	➤ impatience	➤ covetousness
➤ hostility	➤ despondency	➤ strife	➤ annoyance	➤ frugality
➤ ill will	➤ dejection	➤ apprehension	➤ irritability	➤ greed
➤ loathing	➤ dysphoria	➤ restlessness	➤ quick tempered	➤ stinginess
➤ scorn	➤ hopelessness	➤ mistrust	➤ rashness	➤ bitterness
➤ spite	➤ moodiness	➤ nervousness	➤ violence	➤ insensitivity

goodness	faithfulness	gentleness	self-control
➤ selfish desire	➤ dishonesty	➤ callousness	➤ self-indulgence
➤ wickedness	➤ disloyalty	➤ rudeness	➤ self-gratification
➤ indecency	➤ betrayal	➤ vulgarity	➤ neglect
➤ anger	➤ deceitfulness	➤ crassness	➤ excess
➤ corruptness	➤ infidelity	➤ smuttiness	➤ permissiveness
➤ destruction	➤ deception	➤ poor taste	➤ squandering
➤ maliciousness	➤ falseness	➤ crudeness	➤ chaos
➤ carelessness	➤ trickery	➤ toughness	➤ confusion

Highlight any words that resonate in your spirit, suggesting you have walked in this fruit of the enemy at some point in your journey. Ask Holy Spirit to bring to your remembrance how you have done so. He will show you the key incidents. Bring them to the Lord in repentance, coming out of partnership with them. ("I repent and remove partnering with…") Ask Holy Spirit if there is any restitution you need to make or anyone you need to forgive for each event. Take your time. It is quite a lengthy process, but it is part of becoming the **sanctified vessel** the Lord requires you to be so He can take you where He has destined you to go. **Record your revelations to help guide your prayer time.**

B. Time for Change

As you come out of alignment with the bitter fruits of the enemy, you will most likely discover some of your lifestyle choices have not been godly. Repentance is the starting point, but the Lord wants you to take it further. He wants you to *renounce* it: turn from it and change the thoughts and behavior patterns. He requires deep change, not simply a continual cycle of producing bitter fruit and then asking for forgiveness. He requires you to break out of the cycle so you can steadily move forward. And once you have victory in an area, you are given the authority to bring healing to others held in the same bondage. You are called to set other captives free, but first, you must be set free yourself. It is time. Though this may be impossible on your own, with God, freedom awaits. You can do this in His strength.

Ask the Lord if there are any specific areas of your lifestyle in which you need to make some changes. Write a prayer of surrender, handing this area over to Him, and allowing Him to do with it as He pleases. Ask for the wisdom and grace you need to make the changes He requires of you.

_____
_____
_____
_____
_____
_____
_____
_____
_____
_____

Write a plan of spiritual warfare for change, asking the Lord for His wisdom and step-by-step guidance that will lead you to be successful in this. Make the plan progressive, starting with small changes and adding to them gradually as you become accustomed to your new choices. Do some research if necessary, to help you develop a sound plan.

Ask the Lord to show you how to avoid the traps of the enemy as he attempts to sabotage your plan. No matter how many times you have failed in the past, as you daily commit it to God, He will be faithful in strengthening you. Do not give up!

Along with the basic tenants of actions to take, your plan of spiritual warfare for change should include a list of daily declarations, and prayer for the Lord's help in walking in the fruit of the Spirit: "Lord, help me to walk in the fruit of Your Spirit. Let love, joy, peace, patience, kindness, goodness, faithfulness, gentleness, and self-control be the witness I show to those around me."

Page 154

Prayer:

I request the honor of praying over you as you set out on this new, exciting journey of healing.

Dear Lord, I bring my friends before You, humbled and honored that you have brought them into my life, in whatever capacity You have chosen to do so. You love them dearly, and You desire them to walk in Your ways, so they can receive everything You have promised them; so they can go everywhere You are leading them. There are so many things in the world that draw us, deceive us, tempt us. But Lord, I pray You put a blinder on my friends that allows them to see and hear You and You alone, that they may bring righteousness to their lifestyle in all manners.

I shut the mouth of the enemy and pull his hands off of their eyes. Blind their eyes, Lord, instead, to the temptations of the enemy. Make them unwavering, steadfast, with a new fortitude rising up with such power that they will know it is You, and this time, it is different—this time, as they draw nearer to You, You will give them the grace and wisdom to do all You ask them to do. They *will* walk in victory so they can be released to set other captives free.

In the name of Jesus, I bind up the spirit of chaos, and ask the Shalom Peace of God to overtake every part of their spirit, soul, and body. Lord, I ask you to reverse all muscle memory that entered during the times of trauma. Let their minds and bodies be in continual peace that comes from You. Rewire their brain and nervous system to operate under this Spirit of peace, corresponding fully to Your original design for them.

I ask You to bring people into their lives to encourage them in their areas of weakness, and neutralize those who would try to discourage them. Increase their faith, and remove any doubt or fear that holds them back from going hard after You and the treasures and authority You hold for them as they walk in righteousness and purity, with clean hands and pure hearts. Make my friends vessels of honor, sanctified vessels, useful for the Master, and prepared for every good work. I pray this in the mighty name of Jesus. Amen.

Thank you, my friends, for allowing me to be a part of your journey. The blessing has been mine.

Jocelyn A Drozda

His Truth

Ask for understanding as you seek the knowledge of the Lord and follow His instruction. Highlight all of the "fruit" of wisdom found in these verses.

My son, if you receive my words,

And treasure my commands within you,

So that you incline your ear to wisdom,

And apply your heart to understanding;

Yes, if you cry out for discernment,

And lift up your voice for understanding,

If you seek her as silver,

And search for her as *for* hidden treasures;

Then you will understand the fear of the LORD,

And find the knowledge of God.

For the LORD gives wisdom;

From His mouth *come* knowledge and understanding;

He stores up sound wisdom for the upright;

He is a shield to those who walk uprightly;

He guards the path of justice,

And preserves the way of His saints.

Then you will understand righteousness and justice,

Equity *and* every good path.

When wisdom enters your heart,

And knowledge is pleasant to your soul,

Discretion will preserve you;

Understanding will keep you…

Proverbs 2:1-11 (NKJV)

My son, do not forget my law,

But let your heart keep my commands;

For length of days and long life

And peace they will add to you.

Let not mercy and truth forsake you;

Bind them around your neck,

Write them on the tablet of your heart,

And so find favor and high esteem

In the sight of God and man.

Do not be wise in your own eyes;

Fear the LORD and depart from evil.

It will be health to your flesh,

And strength to your bones.

The LORD by wisdom founded the earth;

By understanding He established the heavens;

By His knowledge the depths were broken up,

And clouds drop down the dew.

My son, let them not depart from your eyes—

Keep sound wisdom and discretion;

So they will be life to your soul

And grace to your neck.

Then you will walk safely in your way,

And your foot will not stumble.

When you lie down, you will not be afraid;

Yes, you will lie down and your sleep will be sweet.

Do not be afraid of sudden terror,

Nor of trouble from the wicked when it comes;

For the LORD will be your confidence,

And will keep your foot from being caught.

Wisdom *is* the principal thing;

Therefore get wisdom.

And in all your getting, get understanding.

Exalt her, and she will promote you;

She will bring you honor, when you embrace her.

She will place on your head an ornament of grace,

A crown of glory she will deliver to you."

Hear, my son, and receive my sayings,

And the years of your life will be many.

I have taught you in the way of wisdom;

I have led you in right paths.

When you walk, your steps will not be hindered,

And when you run, you will not stumble.

My son, give attention to my words;

Incline your ear to my sayings.

Do not let them depart from your eyes;

Keep them in the midst of your heart;

For they *are* life to those who find them,

And health to all their flesh.

Proverbs 3:1-4, 7, 8, 19-26, Proverbs 4:7-12, 20-22 (NKJV)

Praying His Truth

Write a prayer thanking the Lord for the blessings He gives us as we follow His wisdom. Focus on the phrases you highlighted.

At the core of the anxiety, depression, fear, unbelief, and all the other bitter fruit with which we continually struggle, lies a deep mistrust, lodged firmly in our hearts by believing all the lies of the enemy for all these years. This mistrust has pushed us out of alignment with the will, desires, and purposes of God for our lives.

Realignment with the Lord and His truth has been the first step. The next step is learning how to stay aligned so you can walk in this truth, in the fulness of power and authority in Christ, and fulfill His plan for your life. This comes through the process of building a stronger, more intimate relationship with the Lord, and understanding His ways, as they are so different from our own. This becomes our firm foundation.

Welcome to Book Three!

My Inward Expressions

As the Lord shows you the truth of who you are, record it on this page.

THE LORD IS ...

As the Lord reveals the truth of who He is, of how He sees you, record it on this page.

I am Found

What is your new self-talk? Highlight the words with which you now identify. Compare your selections with those in Book One. Celebrate your healing!

- visible
- unmasked
- confident
- noticed
- seen
- unveiled
- known
- significant
- God's child
- fully developed
- enough
- irreplaceable
- chosen
- invited
- not forgotten
- consequential
- more than
- forgiving
- creative
- loving
- free
- hopeful
- patient

- important
- valued
- fully realized
- valuable
- needed
- accepted
- honored
- treasured
- cherished
- worthwhile
- worthy
- fully qualified
- surrounded
- loved
- lovable
- not silent
- worth pursuing
- peaceful
- beautiful
- strong
- graceful
- compassionate
- thankful

- princess/prince
- warrior
- king/queen
- overcomer
- heir
- royalty
- gentle
- wise
- appreciated
- smart
- generous
- courageous
- brave
- faithful
- loyal
- joyful
- forgiven
- honoring
- truthful
- honest
- dynamic
- godly
- righteous

My Declaration

Write your declaration of God's truth of who He created you to be as revealed throughout the course of your healing journey to this point. Review the pages of this journal, where you poured out your heart, and the Father poured His heart into you, to remind yourself of these truths. Post this page in a place where you will see it often, and speak its words of truth over yourself daily.

Fully Armed: Worksheet

Partner with Holy Spirit as you use the weapons of warfare to break down enemy walls as new situations arise and wounds occur in your life. Refer back to the manual when needed. Use each section relevant to your situation.

Revealing Targets
What hurts? What is aggravating you?

Walking in Repentance
Repent and turn from any connected ungodly thoughts, actions, and behaviors.
"I repent and renounce ..."

Breaking Free
Are you operating in any unholy spirits such as anger, pride, jealousy, rebellion ...
"I bind up and cast off the spirit of _____ in Jesus' name. I come out of alignment with it. I will no longer partner with it in any manner."

Shedding the Mentality
Are you holding on to any protective personalities?
"I release the protective personality of _____ from my life. I will not partner with it any longer. It is not a part of my God-given identity. I will instead trust in ..."

© Healing Identity/J.A. Drozda (Copy permission granted for individual and group healing and instructional purposes.)

Removing Targets & Realigning with God's Truth

What lies are you believing? *"I come out of alignment with the lie that ..."*
What inner vows have you made? *"I cancel the vow that ..."*
"God's truth is ..."

Finding Jesus

"Where were you, Jesus?"

Letting Go

What do you need to surrender to the Lord?

Forgiveness

Do you need to forgive someone or ask for forgiveness? Do you need to make restitution?

© Healing Identity/J.A. Drozda (Copy permission granted for individual and group healing and instructional purposes.)

Grieving Losses

What have you lost in this situation? What is grieving your heart? Pour it out to the Lord. Let the healing tears wash your soul.

Practicing Gratefulness

"Thank You, Lord, for ..."

Moving Forward (praying for vision)

What do you need to reclaim or have the Lord restore? (Hope, dreams, vision, peace, joy, relationships, finances, your body/soul/spirit ...)

"Lord, I ask you to restore to me ..."
"In Jesus' name I reclaim ..."

Seeking Revelation

"Lord, fill me with Your love, mercy, grace, and peace. What would You say to my heart right now?"

© Healing Identity/J.A. Drozda (Copy permission granted for individual and group healing and instructional purposes.)

Healing Testimony

And they have conquered sin by the blood of the Lamb and by the word of their testimony…

Revelation 12:11

If you wish to share your healing testimony, write your story here, snap a picture, and email it to jdrozda@myaccess.ca. Feel free to share any significant journal pages!

Prophetic Voices

Maryann Ward
Author/Illustrator of *Olivia & Me*
Event Speaker
Contact - maryann@maward.ca

Tanya Foster
Prophetic Team Member
Life Group Leader

Diane Harrison
Author of *The Power of Prophetic Teams* and *Prophetic Team Workbook*
Leader of Prophetic Ministries at Harvest City Church, Regina, Sk, Canada
Contact - www.dianeharrison.ca

Recommended Reading

Linwood, Calli
Coming Through the Fire: Preparing for Battle

Reid, Kimm
Realigned: Bringing God's Promises from Heaven to Earth

Reid, Kimm
Life Laid Down: Dare to Live Unordinary, Unstoppable, Unlimited

All books available on www.amazon.com

Endnotes

[1] *St. Irenaeus of Lyons*. Crossroad Initiative. https://www.crossroadsinitiative.com (accessed February 16, 2018)
[2] Michael Dye. *The Genesis Process.* https://www.genesisprocess.org (accessed December 10, 2017)
[3] Linwood, Calli J. *Break Forth*. Helena: Ahelia Publishing Inc, 2017
[4] Cleansing Stream Ministries, Canada. https://www.cleansingstream.ca (accessed February 22, 2018)

What people are saying about Invisible No More

➤ "My friend talked me into coming to Jocelyn's workshop. I had no clue I would be so impacted by *Invisible No More—Healing Relational Perspectives*. The Lord has taken me on a journey of healing and a deeper understanding of how much I'm loved. My journey has just begun; I'm excited to continue down the path of healing and learning who God intended me to be. (D. Godwin)

➤ "For my entire life, I had always thought of myself as fat. As I delved into the self-hatred section in chapter two (*Personal Identity Restored*), I fully expected my fat self-image was at its root. But while exploring this subject, I was shockingly led to an early childhood memory of sexual experimentation with a much older teen of the same sex. After digging deeper, I realized that hating myself for being fat disguised the underlying reason why I hated myself—how dirty, guilty, and shameful I felt because of this sexual stuff. I had believed I had dealt with that area earlier in my Christian walk, but God took me even deeper and I received a greater measure of freedom for the many interconnected issues that have followed me my entire life. Wow! It certainly wasn't what I expected when I cracked open Book Two, but I'm glad God led me to see the true root behind the life-long self-hatred."

➤ "One thing I gained from the workshop for *Invisible No More—Healing Relational Perspectives* was learning how to listen to God's voice and knowing I can hear Him speaking to me."

➤ "I am on my second time through Book One and I am still getting more out of it."

➤ "Through *Invisible No More—Personal Identity Restored*, I came to understand how the enemy of our souls uses fear to keep us from fulfilling our destiny. Even our aversions to certain situations can be a clue as to areas he tries to keep us from entering into. With each fear that is cut off, a new door of opportunity opens up. I have lost much due to fear, doubt, and intimidation, but through this book, God has shown me how to step out of fear and into His purposes for me."

➤ "The workbook is an excellent guide to work with on my own time. I liked working one-on-one with Holy Spirit during the program. I know more of the truth and the lies I have been told and believed for too long."

➤ "This has been an amazing journey; I never expected this workshop would take me so deep into my heart. I have gained a deeper understanding of how much the Lord loves me and how the enemy's lies were overpowering the love of God."

Book Three

Identity in Christ: Aligned with Destiny

Book Three—Identity in Christ: Aligned with Destiny

Unit One—Words in the Hand (Speak words of life)

Unit Two—Going Up (Practicing gratefulness and worship)

Unit Three—Cliff Jumping (Trust and obedience)

Unit Four—Out of the Box (Knowing the Father's Heart)

Unit Five—Time Traps (Distractions and Idols)

Unit Six—Walking in His Ways (Spiritual Disciplines)

Unit Seven—Your Isaac Moment (God's Testing)